National Interscholastic Athletic Administrators Association

Dear Friends,

The National Interscholastic Athletic Administrators Association (NIAAA) is a professional organization dedicated to the promotion and facilitation of interscholastic athletics in the educational system that is vital to young people. In addition, the NIAAA is the primary provider of services and education for athletic administrators who conduct these programs. The benefits of participation opportunities for student-athletes are immeasurable for their growth and development into adulthood.

Likewise, Athletes for a Better World (ABW) was formed to utilize sports as a developer of character, teamwork, and citizenship through commitment to a *Code for Living* application for life. The NIAAA is pleased to join with ABW to provide this special NIAAA edition of *Winning More Than The Game* to administrators, coaches, parents, students, and supporters of high school athletics across the country.

The NIAAA Student Scholarship/Essay competition recognizes distinguished high school student athletes in the attribute areas of scholastics, leadership, citizenship, participation, volunteerism and the importance of school sports participation in the student's life. *The Code for Living* criteria have been incorporated into the scholarship application by asking applicants to reflect upon the tenets of life lessons learned through sport and how they relate and impact their life. This book challenges readers to consider the *Code for Living* via exercises, as a springboard for life qualities of character development.

The NIAAA and ABW partnership includes annually recognizing one male and one female national NIAAA scholarship winner as automatic recipients of the prestigious Coach Wooden Citizenship Cup. These two high school athletes will join two collegiate winners and a professional recipient each year as exemplary role models of the *Code for Living*. Please join us in supporting education-based athletic programs. May each of us recognize the responsibility to support young people in their learning, development and participation; commit to personally reflect the same qualities and to always share the best attributes afforded youth development through athletics.

Sincerely,

Bruce Whitehead, CMAA
NIAAA Executive Director

WHAT THEY HAVE SAID ....

"Sport is only a part of our lives. The Code for Living isn't just good for those of us who are professional athletes; it's good for kids and parents of all ages."
— Peyton Manning, Denver Broncos

"ABW's philosophy about sports is very similar to mine. We believe that there are many life lessons that can be learned through sports, and that, when taught properly, sports can help us grow on and off the field. Winning More Than The Game is valuable for athletes, coaches, and parents, and ABW's mission to make everyone stronger through sports is one we can all learn from."
— Cal Ripken, Jr., Baseball Hall of Fame

"ABW is working to create the proper values and environment in sports for our young people to grow up in. The Code for Living is needed at every level of sports today."
— Tom Glavine, former pitcher, Atlanta Braves

"One's true character is refined in the heat of competition. We must help our athletes develop their core identities on the playing field and in life."
— Danielle M. Donehew, Executive Director, Women's Basketball Coaches Association, and Member of Board of Directors, Athletes for a Better World

"The ABW tenets of sportsmanship are critical in the development of the total person as we seek to build character in today's student-athletes on a daily basis."
— Tommy Marshall, Athletic Director, Marist School, Atlanta
Former Chair, National Interscholastic Athletic Administrators Association

"The Code for Living provides the kind of good, sound advice that guides and inspires students long after they have graduated from school....you have a partner in the Seattle Schools."

— Joseph Olchefske, former Superintendent, Seattle Public Schools

"Your Code for Living makes a simple job of effectively applying morals in a team atmosphere. Thanks for all your support of coaches who truly care about their players, and not just the outcome of the game."

— Janine Sullivan, soccer coach, Milford, OH

"Your work is so very important and The Boys' Club New York is proud to be a member of your team."

— Brad Zervas, Boys' Club of New York

"I already have the Board of the Weston Soccer Club excited and ready to join. This is FANTASTIC stuff... GREAT WORK!"

— Ken Bresnahan, Weston Soccer Club, Weston, FL

"As a current player in the Arena Football League and a high school teacher/coach, I can appreciate the Code for Living on both ends."

— Lance Funderburk, QB, Arizona Rattlers

"Our program is honored to be a part of ABW."

— Marcia Foster, Assistant coach, women's basketball team,
California Polytechnic State University

"We like the simple, positive, and comprehensive nature of the Code. It tries to raise the bar of behavior for all of us."

— Rick Skirvin, Georgia State Soccer Association Executive Director

"Every kid should grow up with the Code for Living."

— Hugh Stephenson, Buckhead Baseball coach, Atlanta, GA

WINNING
MORE
THAN THE GAME

FRED NORTHUP

ISBN-10: 151535668X
EAN-13: 9781515356684

Dedication

This book is written in thanksgiving for all that the world of sports has brought to my life, from the earliest games of my youth, to the lessons and relationships I continue to gain. This book is dedicated to the future, that what begins as the fun of childhood may always lead us to discover and nurture the best in us. My thanks to the board and friends of Athletes for a Better World whose support has made possible these efforts of mine over the past seventeen years. And my appreciation and abiding love to Julie, my teammate of over 40 years, whose patience and insight have always made better any ideas I have.

—FBN

Athletes for a Better World

Athletes for a Better World (ABW) began in 1998 with the goal of changing the culture of sport in America. By developing The Code for Living, the ABW vision was to articulate the positive values that have historically been the foundation of good sportsmanship and good citizenship, and then to challenge individuals, teams, and leagues to commit to The Code, providing support and resources to those who joined the effort. Since its founding, ABW has spread to virtually every state and to several foreign countries. Every week more than 3,000 coaches, athletic directors, and league officials receive the Tip of the Week, a three-minute teaching lesson for those working with youth. Sign up at www.abw.org.

ATHLETES
FOR A BETTER
WORLD

Who will benefit from reading Winning More Than the Game?

- Amateur and professional athletes
- Parents, guardians and mentors
- Sports-management students
- Sports agents
- Participants in character education or life-skills courses
- Amateur and professional league or conference executives
- College and high school administrators
- Camp and recreation club/center counselors
- School PE administrators
- Church-league athletes and coaches

Table of Contents

Foreword

In 2003 after I had retired from coaching but was still Athletic Director of the University of Georgia, I received a message from a retired Episcopal priest named Fred Northup who wanted to meet with me to solicit my support for an organization called "Athletes for a Better World."

It sounded like a noble cause but, quite frankly, I had received a lot of requests to support worthy causes that, unfortunately, I was not always able to honor. This message got my attention fast, however, when it further stated that the aim of the organization was to change the culture of sportsmanship (that had gone astray) and to enhance the character of the participants by recognizing positive athletic role models with the inspiration of Coach John Wooden as the focal point.

Coach Wooden was one of my greatest heroes and role models both as a coach and as a person. Sportsmanship and character were at the top of his priorities and consequently mine as well. I was anxious to learn more. After meeting with him, I was convinced this former Dean of St. Mark's Cathedral in Seattle, Washington, was committed to the ideals he espoused and had the drive and determination to make it happen. I lent my support to the cause that day by joining the Board, and since that time, more than a decade later, I have been the beneficiary of a renewed spirit of the values of character and sportsmanship. As the Chair of the Wooden Cup Advisory Committee, it is inspiring each year to learn of the remarkable stories behind the professional, collegiate, and most recently, high school athletes who receive the Coach Wooden Citizenship Cup.

Fred (we are soul brothers now) has provided us all with a wonderful gift in his book <u>Winning More Than The Game</u>. He has used all of his lifetime experiences, as a priest, teacher, coach, student, and athlete in writing this book superbly outlining his "Code for Living." These positive role model principles summarize the athlete's responsibility as an individual, as a member of a team, and as a member of society. In a short period of time this code has acquired legs and has spread throughout this country and into several countries abroad. This book will further spread the value and lessons of the "Code for Living" to all athletes, at all levels, for many lifetimes to come. It is a treasured gift. Thanks, Fred, for sharing it with us.

Vincent J. Dooley
Member, College Football Hall of Fame
Former Athletic Director, University of Georgia
Chair, Coach Wooden Citizenship Cup Advisory Committee

Introduction from the Author

I am a teacher.

I identify with legendary UCLA basketball coach John Wooden, who always said that he considered himself primarily a teacher, with the gym as the classroom. I have spent many hours teaching in an actual classroom setting, but whether I am coaching a young athlete, painting a house, or moving a grand piano, it is in my nature to want to "show someone" how to do things.

I founded Athletes for a Better World in 1998. As it turns out, this work has brought together all the years of education, training, and experience that I have had as an athlete, student, teacher, coach, Episcopal priest, and counselor. I was convinced to write this book because I have been asked many times to publish the things I have said and taught. It brings together the core values that I believe we all should share as human beings, as well as the steps we need to take to reach our full potential as individuals, members of a community, and citizens of our country. This book is placed in the context of sports, but I am teaching what I have learned about life.

It's better to have character than to be a character.
— John Wooden, UCLA head basketball coach

It's better to be a good person than a good player.

— Archie Manning, former NFL quarterback

GROWING UP

I was born in Asheville, North Carolina, in 1945. When I was five years old I learned how to ride a bicycle in one afternoon. (Here's how to do it: Sit on the bike, put one foot on the bottom step of any building, push off, go a few feet, crash. Repeat until successful; bike will be dented with many scratches, and so will you, but you won't care.) I remember riding my bike, playing football and baseball in the street, and taking tennis, horseback riding, and swimming lessons. But I played in no organized sports, just various pickup games with my friends. Every day we picked teams, made up the rules, and learned to play together. The school I went to had no sports at all, just recess.

When I was eleven we moved to Connecticut, where our house was one block from the Boys Club. I played basketball and baseball and learned to shoot pool, but there were no coaches or organized teams. I learned to sail at the local sailing club and sailed in weekly races on Long Island Sound. A beginning sailor, I almost always came in last place.

In all of these various sports of my boyhood, I had the same experience we all do in one way or another: of beginning something, getting better at it, and finally becoming "good" at it in some sense. It is this experience—learned through desire, discipline, work, patience, and results—that we all have in differing ways.

During my high school years at Brooks School in Massachusetts, being an athlete was an important part of my identity, and I practiced many hours alone to improve my skills. For example, in the spring of my sophomore year, as soon as basketball season was over, I started practicing for the next year. I remember going to the gym every day for about 30 minutes on my way to tennis practice and shooting only left-handed layups, hooks, and short shots. The best players could all shoot close to the basket with both hands, and I wanted to be one of the best.

Our values become instilled within us at a young age. I gained much from my parents and the headmaster, teachers, and coaches at Brooks, which I attended from the eighth grade through high school.

I was formed in many ways during these years, and the joys of sport and athletic competition were an important part of my life there. Some of my fondest memories are of chasing a soccer ball all afternoon on a glorious fall day, and of doing basketball drills in a chilly gym with the snow piling up outside while enjoying the encouraging spirit of our coach. But the values that stand behind Athletes for a Better World are in large measure those that I learned from Frank Ashburn, the headmaster of Brooks, and that were reinforced daily on the playing field by all our coaches.

It may seem odd that the great truths about sport and athletic competition were learned from the headmaster, but Mr. Ashburn's influence was all-pervasive. He set the tone for the school by his words and presence. Exhortations to decency, manners, respect, and integrity were our common fare from him. It was Mr. Ashburn who would launch into two-minute sermonettes on topics such as honor, fair play, giving one's best, team play and the common good, or the spirit of the law versus the letter of the law. He often used the athletic arena as examples for his words and wisdom about life.

Today, as then, it seems unimaginable that anyone could lecture us on these topics of virtue and expect us to listen. But Mr. Ashburn could. Because of his own inherent integrity and moral force, he was able to challenge us to become more than we were. In those little spontaneous talks, usually inspired by someone's delinquency, he would raise the moral bar for each of us on what it meant to be a person. In addition to his learnedness and iconic figure, he had a dry and ever-engaging wit.

The coaches adhered to the same values Mr. Ashburn embraced. Other schools might, for example, exhibit poor sportsmanship, but that would never be tolerated by any coach I knew. It would be unthinkable to show up an opponent, talk back to an official, or lose your temper. If you did, you would not only have to face your coach, but you might well find yourself hearing Mr. Ashburn remind you of his expectations for you.

At Brooks I played on some good teams, such as the soccer team, but we also had many losing teams. With that, we learned to face disappointment and defeat—on a regular basis! "How do you respond to failure?" was one of Mr. Ashburn's regular themes. Would we respond by sulking, complaining, giving up? Or by working harder, learning from mistakes, and trying again? The basketball team I captained (one of the worst in the history of the school) was an ongoing laboratory in experiencing defeat. At the same time, our coaches were models of patience, kindness, commitment, and of the perspective that it was only a game.

> How do you respond to failure? Would we respond by sulking, complaining, giving up? Or by working harder, learning from mistakes, and trying again?

As a nation today, we are consumed with winning. The slogan of Athletes for a Better World, "Winning More Than The Game," is a reflection of the values I learned at Brooks. Athletics were never about winning at all costs. It was more the Greek ideal: the opportunity to develop one's skills, to train one's body, to learn what it is to be a part of a team, to play within the rules of the sport, to go all out and to give one's best effort to try to win. Competition was the opportunity to test one's skills and the skills of the team against an opponent, and to learn from the experience. (Mr. Ashburn would read Rudyard Kipling's If each year in chapel, and he would often remind us that mature adults could and would "meet with triumph and disaster and treat those two imposters just the same.")

> Competition was the opportunity to test one's skills and the skills of the team against an opponent, and to learn from the experience.

Grantland Rice is perhaps best remembered for writing, "the One Great Scorer...marks not that you won nor lost, but how you played the game." That was the philosophy we grew up with; not that it didn't matter (Rice never said that), but that something mattered more than the final score—how you played the game. And Mr. Ashburn made it plain that the game was not just the contest itself but how you practiced; what kind of teammate you were; how you carried yourself; and how you treated those two imposters, triumph and disaster.

Mr. Ashburn also often spoke about duty and civic responsibility. Over and over again he would remind us that we were not put on this earth for the purpose of feathering our own nest, but for somehow making the world a better place, for living a responsible life. My father and mother emphasized these values as well. This is why understanding our civic duty is central to my work with Athletes for a Better World. Through The Code for Living, our vision is to provide the framework for sports, sportsmanship, and civic responsibility that I learned and experienced growing up, because these are the things that transfer into our lives and make us successful and able to develop to our full potential.

When the One Great Scorer comes to mark beside your name, He marks not that you won nor lost, but how you played the game.
— Grantland Rice, sportswriter

In college, I was briefly on the tennis team, played all the intramural sports, and studied political science in Paris my junior year. After graduating, my first job was as a French teacher at the McCallie School in Chattanooga, Tennessee, where I had my first experiences as a high school teacher and coach. Later, I would teach (at one time or another) every age from kindergarten through college and beyond, and, like many parents, coach various youth sports. It is surprising to realize that I have taught, coached, and been a mentor to children and young people of every age for over 50 years.

We are what we repeatedly do. Excellence, then, is not an act but a habit.
— Aristotle, Greek philospher

Toward the end of 1997 I had lunch with Michael Campbell, who was then the head of the Sports and Events Council in Seattle. Only a few days before, Latrell Sprewell, an NBA player with the Golden State Warriors, had tried to choke his coach, P.J. Carlesimo. I was discussing with Campbell what direction my future career would take. After 25 years in the ordained ministry, I wanted to return to my love of sports. He said to me, "There are a lot of things you can do, Fred, but if you could get these guys to grow up and behave, the world would love it." Although the details would change over the coming months, it was from that moment that the idea for Athletes for a Better World was born.

Frederick B. Northup
June 2011

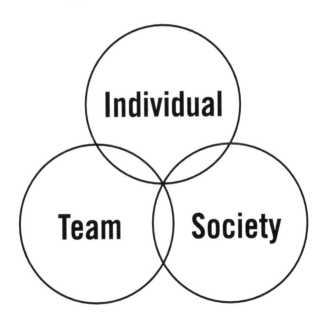

CHAPTER 1

Introducing The Code for Living

THE FIRST STEPS

Before I founded Athletes for a Better World (ABW), I thought about how much I had benefited as a young man from my experiences in sport. I had caring coaches and teachers who made sure that I developed my athletic abilities but at the same time kept all things in perspective.

From growing up in sports, I had learned the great values of discipline, hard work, teamwork, and the sense of pride and accomplishment that improvement brought, as well as learning to play as a team. I experienced the joy of winning and the pain of losing. Robert Fulghum may have learned everything he needed to know in kindergarten, but I learned everything I needed to know on the athletic fields. The Duke of Wellington said that "the battle of Waterloo was won on the playing fields of Eton," a school in England. What he meant was that the character, determination, and teamwork learned in high school sports at Eton is what "won the battle" years later at Waterloo. I wanted to pass on to future young athletes all the important lessons I had learned as a young man so that future young athletes would learn how to win the battles of life through their sports experiences.

The Battle of Waterloo was won on the playing fields of Eton.
— The Duke of Wellington

When I look out at the landscape of sports, I see a different world at every level—youth sports, high school, college, and professional—than the one in which I grew up. We see win-at-all-costs coaches, out-of-control parents, greedy owners of professional teams, egotistical professional athletes, drugs, steroids, gambling, and myriad other problems that fill the sports pages on a daily basis.

Like so many who have seriously lamented the current state of affairs, I began to wonder, how do you begin to swim upstream against this culture? As I pondered that question, I came to the conclusion that I needed to put down on paper the principal values that I had learned as a child, those that I thought should be a part of every sport and that also would carry over into life. To test my own ideas, I set out to interview a number of friends in the field of athletics and asked them all a simple question: What are the important values that you think a person should learn from participating in sports that will enable that person to become the best person that he or she can be?

DEVELOPING THE CODE FOR LIVING

I took notes from everyone I interviewed and later tried to group all of the similar responses together. I soon realized that some of the responses had to do with the person as an individual, others with the person as a member of a team, and still others with the person as a member of society. Combining my own experiences with the responses that I had been given, I wrote and re-wrote what became The Code for Living. In writing The Code, I also drew on my own experiences off the field. I have listened to people whose jobs have grown frustrating or boring, or whose bosses are not people they like or admire. I have counseled couples whose marriages are crumbling because of some choices they made, and with young people trying to determine who they are and who they will be. I have heard the stories of failure, of the desire to end a job, a marriage, even a life.

One of the things I learned long ago is that it is far easier to understand the problems of others (or to see the changes they need to make) than it is to enable them to see the problems or convince them to make the changes. Telling a person what their problem is does not usually help. Leading them to the point where they can see it for themselves is usually necessary before any real change can begin to occur.

While my background is steeped in the Judeo-Christian traditions, the values of The Code are appropriate to all people, of any faith tradition or of no faith tradition.

The Code is not intended as a set of suggestions, a group of possibilities, or a nice way to behave. It is written as a commitment to certain values and behaviors.

The Code was deliberately written in first person ("I will") because it is not a series of suggestions but a series of commitments. It is an articulation of what "I am going to do," not of what would be a "good thing" to do. It is an active, not a passive, statement of "who I want to be." The Code is not intended as a set of ideas, a group of possibilities, or a nice way to behave. It is written as a commitment to certain values and behaviors. The preamble includes the phrase "I will take responsibility... when I fail to live up to this Code." So, we acknowledge from the beginning that none of us is perfect and that we will all make mistakes. Nevertheless, the form of The Code is creedal. It is articulating clearly how we intend to behave; it is a commitment that we intend to live by. My goal in creating The Code was to articulate the core values that I thought we should all be able to agree on, and then to challenge everyone involved in sports at any level to live by this code.

THE CODE FOR LIVING
LIFE LESSONS LEARNED THROUGH SPORTS

Because I am a role model and have the opportunity and responsibility to make a difference in the lives of others, I commit to this Code. I will take responsibility and appropriate actions when I fail to live up to it.

As an Individual:

- I will develop my skills to the best of my ability and give my best effort in practice and competition.
- I will compete within the spirit and letter of the rules of my sport.
- I will respect the dignity of every human being, and will not be abusive or dehumanizing of another either as an athlete or as a fan.

As a Member of a Team:

- I will place team goals ahead of personal goals.
- I will be a positive influence on the relationships on the team.
- I will follow the team rules established by the coach.

As a Member of Society:

- I will display caring and honorable behavior off the field and be a positive influence in my community and world.

- I will give of my time, skills, and money as I am able for the betterment of my community and world.

THE IMPORTANCE OF THE CODE

My old high school edition of Webster's dictionary defines "code" as "any system of principles or rules." Codes are important in our lives. They surround us in written and unwritten forms. The written ones are such things as the laws by which we live, the religious creeds or affirmations that we make, the oaths and mottos we take as part of social, service, and scouting organizations, as well as the mission statements that are a part of corporate America. There are many unwritten but clearly understood codes at home, at work, and on the street. We all know to be quiet when we enter a house of worship, a public library, or a movie theater. We know to show respect to an older person and to be nice to pets. Many of us grew up in homes that had understood expectations and duties for all of us—to wash our hands before eating, clean up our rooms, and so on.

ABW's Code for Living is intended to be a unifying set of principles around which people of all ages and sports interests can join together. It is not intended to replace any of the written or unwritten codes of one's religion, family, or work, but it strives to provide unity, focus, support, and direction to those who participate in sports.

In less than three years, The Code for Living spread to virtually every state, and several countries overseas. It was endorsed by school superintendents, park and recreation departments, Boys and Girls Clubs, YMCAs, and sports leaders throughout the country.

After The Code was written, the question became, what would it be called? We settled on "The Code for Living" because that is exactly what it is, not just a set of values for young athletes, but a set of principles by which we all should live. No matter who you are, we wanted to create a value system that you would recognize as valuable to you.

ABW is working to create the proper values and environment in sports for our young people to grow up in.

The Code for Living is needed at every level of sports today.
— Tom Glavine, former MLB pitcher

THE PREAMBLE

Because I am a role model and have the opportunity and responsibility to make a difference in the lives of others, I commit to this Code. I will take responsibility and appropriate actions when I fail to live up to it.

The preamble begins with the recognition that we do not live in isolation but are a part of the human family with the opportunity and the responsibility to make a difference in the lives of others. In other words, we have a moral obligation to behave in certain ways as members of society. It also recognizes that we will all fail to give our best at times, and when that occurs, we must summon the courage to take responsibility and appropriate action. What is appropriate, of course, will depend on the situation.

I AM A ROLE MODEL

Professional athletes like to talk about who is and who is not a role model. Charles Barkley famously said, "I am not a role model." What he meant is that, as an adult professional athlete, he is not responsible for the behavior of young children. He may not want to be a role model, but he is whether he likes it or not. The truth is that we are all role models—every one of us. If we watch a children's soccer game and see a young child have a temper tantrum, we make judgments both about that child and about the child's parents. That child is a role model, for better or for worse, for all those watching. We are all role models for each other. The ways we behave or misbehave, act or react, are observed by those around us. We are continuously evaluating the behaviors of others and consciously or subconsciously deciding that we approve or disapprove of their behaviors. Indeed, we are continuously formed and re-formed as we observe and react to those around us. The French writer André Malraux wrote a short story about a young man who noticed that a pretty young girl was riding the same bus each day as he. The young man gradually began combing his hair, shining his shoes, checking his clothes, and overall improving his looks even though they never spoke!

We all have the opportunity to make a difference in the lives of others. Who of us cannot think of those special people who have made a difference in our lives: a big brother or sister, a neighbor, a teacher, a coach, or a family friend? Each day presents us with countless opportunities to offer a kind word, to encourage another person, and to somehow brighten the day of another. Of course, in addition to those situations that come to us, countless opportunities arise for us to take the initiative to better another person's life. We all know a person who is ill, in between jobs, grieving the loss of a friend or relative, or worrying about a child or an elderly person approaching the end of life. Will we call them? Will we visit them? The opportunities are always before us.

TAKING RESPONSIBILITY

Most of the opportunities just described are options available to us. But it is our responsibility to act on them. Responsibility is a big word. One of the ways people's character can be measured is by their willingness to take responsibility for their shortcomings or failures. We all know how easy it is to make excuses or pass off blame when something goes wrong. People who take responsibility and acknowledge their own mistakes or limitations are those for whom our respect increases.

> One of the ways people's character can be measured is by their willingness to take responsibility for their shortcomings or failures.

Taking responsibility does not just mean doing the things that we are supposed to do. It also means making sure that others do the things that they are supposed to do. As adults, it is our responsibility to be sure that our children are fed and clothed, that they do their homework, that they arrive on time to the places they are supposed to be, and that they are well-mannered. When other peoples' children are in our charge, it is our responsibility to see that their behaviors reflect the values of their parents. When we are around our peers, it is our responsibility to be certain that other adults are treated fairly and with respect. As adults, and as citizens of this country, it is our responsibility to vote and to support laws that provide for the common good. As we go about our daily lives, we can choose to make this world a better place or choose not to. We can pick up a piece of paper on the street or leave it. We can speak a kind word to a person or say nothing. In other words, we can choose to make a difference each day—even in small but meaningful ways—in the lives of others (such as speaking to someone) or in our community (such as picking up a piece of paper). As children, we want everything for ourselves without regard for others, but a part of growing up is learning that we have opportunities and responsibilities to help others.

It usually takes courage to do the right thing, far more courage than doing nothing or looking the other way.

The preamble also says that we will take responsibility when we fail. It's important to see that there are situations when we can do nothing (if we look the other way, nothing will ever happen to us), or we can take responsibility. When we take responsibility for the mistakes we have made, we take the opportunity to apologize and to make appropriate restitution, such as paying for something we have broken. In this way, we set things right, and we will feel better inside because we know we have done the right thing. It is like a broken bone. If we ignore it, it will not heal properly, but if we acknowledge it and take proper steps, then it can heal well. We can also take responsibility for things that are not our fault and try to set things right. This may involve, for example, trying to get others to acknowledge their mistakes and to take appropriate action. Taking responsibility involves having real courage. It usually takes courage to do the right thing, far more courage than doing nothing or looking the other way. Yet, we all know how much better we feel when we take responsibility and do the right thing, no matter how hard it may be at the time.

THE THREE SECTIONS

The Code has three sections outlining how we will behave as individuals, as members of a team, and as members of society. Just as the Pledge of Allegiance unites Americans in a common bond, whenever a group of people share the same code, it provides the basis for a common vision and purpose. It also provides a basis for knowing what we can expect from each other. Thus, The Code becomes the basis for trust and for group solidarity.

As an Individual

- The Code provides a standard against which each of us can measure ourselves. When we review the tenets of The Code, we can determine the areas we need to improve and then develop personalized strategies for improvement. The values that stand behind The Code for Living are values on which we can all improve—all our lives. At one point in our lives we may need to work on having better discipline in our work habits. At another time, we may want to work on our relationships with others. At still another time, we may want to make greater contributions to our communities. While The Code provides a clear framework, we have the freedom to focus on different elements within it according to our ages, gifts, and circumstances. Therefore, how we choose to live it out will be a challenge that will require constant reflection, with new goals set for ourselves as each year passes.

As a Member of a Team

- The Code is important for us as teammates. We are all on more than one team all the time: the family team, the work team, the neighborhood team, the school team, and even the national team because as citizens of this country we are all on the same team.

- The Code provides a common set of values on which the team can build and grow. Teams are made up of individuals, and yet a team only emerges when the individuals come together in support of common goals. The Code provides the foundation stones on which a true team can be built. The Code recognizes that we have a collective responsibility for one another and for our teams. We need each other and can only be successful with each other. In other words, no one person can make a team. The Code represents a commitment to the team itself. When we share The Code, each person knows what he or she can expect from the other. That knowledge builds confidence and promotes team spirit.

As a Member of Society

- The Code is important because it acknowledges the responsibility we all have as members of society, and it represents a commitment to the betterment of our communities and world. The Code makes it clear what our values are and challenges others to follow suit. It is always important for people who share common values to stand together, and by doing so, to provide an example for others to emulate.

When you know who you are, you know how to act.

IN THE FOLLOWING CHAPTERS

The French philosopher Montaigne said, "Our duty is not to compose books but our character, and to win peace, not in war but in our lives. Our great and glorious accomplishment is to live the right way."

This book is about composing our character. I believe that if we know who we are, we will know how to act, so the development of our own character is the most important work we do. Developing our character will not only lead to personal happiness and success, but it will influence everyone with whom we come into contact. One of the greatest compliments ever made to anyone can be found on the memorial to William Wilberforce in Westminster Abbey. It reads in part: "In an age and country fertile in great and good men, he was among the foremost of those who fixed the character of our times…" What higher or greater compliment could there ever be? He was one of those who "fixed the character of their times!"

Let us turn, then, to the composing of our character. In the following chapters we will look at each of the eight tenets of The Code in detail, providing commentary, lessons, and stories to make the values come alive and accessible for each person.

Throughout the book, you will see reference to the "playbook" as a stopping point for personal reflection or discussion. You are asked to keep a playbook (personal diary) in any form you choose (paper notebook, computer file, etc.) and to then determine the "next steps." This is truly where the work of The Code for Living begins. Meditating upon the questions or topics is the first step toward making real behavior change. These journal entries will become the foundation upon which you will build your character. Play with them. Rewrite them. Reread them. Reconsider them. Your positive momentum will fuel your motivation to continue to the next tenet in The Code for Living.

CHAPTER 2

Living The Code as an Individual

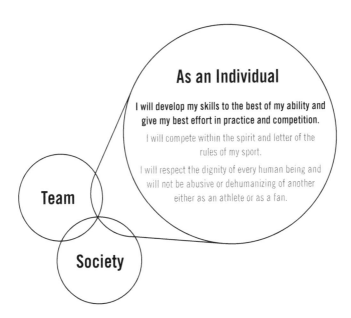

As an Individual

I will develop my skills to the best of my ability and give my best effort in practice and competition.

I will compete within the spirit and letter of the rules of my sport.

I will respect the dignity of every human being and will not be abusive or dehumanizing of another either as an athlete or as a fan.

Team

Society

THE FIRST TENET

In Chapter 2, we will break down the two elements of this tenet and discuss how they comprise the foundation for The Code for Living.

The chapter is organized this way:

"I will develop my skills to the best of my ability..."
2.1 Knowing and Accepting Your Skills and Limitations
2.2 Short-term and Long-term Goals
    Setting Goals Is Linked to Our Self-image
    Setting Goals Is Part of Our Responsibility as Teammates
    Setting Goals Is a Reflection on Those We Represent
    How to Set and Achieve Our Goals
    The Secret to Success: ABW's "Rule of Threes"
    The Big "Mo"

"... and give my best effort in practice and competition."
2.3 Work Ethic
2.4 Self-discipline

"I WILL DEVELOP MY SKILLS TO THE BEST OF MY ABILITY..."

2.1 KNOWING AND ACCEPTING YOUR SKILLS AND LIMITATIONS

In "I will develop my skills...," the key word is "my." Each of us has been given our own set of gifts and talents. Who of us has not wished that we were smarter, better looking, faster, quicker, funnier, taller, shorter, more musical, or more skilled in 1,000 different ways than we are? The first challenge we all face is to accept the skill set we have, to embrace it, and to be enthusiastic in our desire to take those skills and develop them to the best of our ability.

A number of years ago my wife and I met President Nixon at the baptism of his grandson born to his daughter Tricia and son-in-law Ed Cox. President Nixon asked my wife how she knew the Coxes. She said, "Ed and my husband, Fred, played tennis together." "Do you play tennis?" asked the president. "Yes, but I'm not very good," she said. "Give it up!" said Nixon. Whether President Nixon meant to be taken seriously doesn't really matter. His reaction reflects a point of view that is worth considering. Should we only pursue those activities at which we can truly excel? Or, should we pursue those activities that give us pleasure even if we know we may never excel? There are those who want to be the best and who are satisfied with nothing less than the best. While that sort of determination is admirable in some ways, it carries the risk of setting unrealistic goals and of leading a life that is always striving and never satisfied. Limiting yourself only to those areas at which you can truly excel may also deprive you of participating in something that gives you satisfaction even though your skills are limited.

The famous actor Charles Dutton grew up on the streets in the worst area of Baltimore. When he was seventeen years old he killed another man in a gang-type fight. He was convicted of manslaughter and sent to prison. After committing other crimes, he one day found himself in solitary confinement with only a book of plays his girlfriend had given him. He read them and was captivated by them. When his time in solitary was up, he asked the warden if he might form a theatre group in the prison. Eventually the warden allowed him to do this. He studied acting while in prison, was supported by those who saw great promise in him, got a degree in theatre, went to Yale School of Drama, and has become one of the great actors of our time. He had a skill he did not know he had, but when he discovered it, he developed it to the best of his ability.

Regardless of skill level, the key to all success is effort. What child has not delighted in the tale of *The Tortoise and the Hare*, or *The Little Engine That Could*? The hare had the gift of speed, but the tortoise had the gift of persistence. The little engine was small but had a big heart and an iron will. These tales are told and retold, because all parents want their children to learn the value of persistence and hard work.

We are the ones who decide what is "the best of my ability." We may be able to fool others, but we should not be able to fool ourselves. We know what kind of effort we have made, and we know what kind of effort we have not made. As John Wooden observed, "Success is peace of mind, which is a direct result of self-satisfaction in knowing you did your best to become the best you are capable of becoming."

> You can fool all of the people some of the time, and some of the people all of the time, but you can't fool all of the people all of the time.
>
> — Abraham Lincoln

When I was a child, Walt Disney made a movie about Davy Crockett. Crockett had a motto, "Be always sure you're right, then go ahead." This saying expresses two goals: First, to weigh the pros and cons of any action, and second, after making a decision, to pursue relentlessly the goal desired. Part of "being sure you're right" is knowing yourself, your gifts and skills as well as your limitations.

PLAYBOOK EXERCISE

- Do you agree that you should only participate in those things at which you are able to excel? Why or why not?
- What are the skills you have that you most value?
- What is the difference between doing your best and being the best?
- Do you agree with Wooden's definition of success? Why or why not?

NEXT STEPS

- Assess those areas in which you are not gifted but that you enjoy.
- What does success in those areas look like?
- What steps do you need to take to reach success in those areas?

2.2 SHORT-TERM AND LONG-TERM GOALS

Goal setting is at the heart of all skill development. Recently, I decided to begin working out in a gym. I hate working out. Running or swimming laps always seems like gerbil activity to me—give me a ball to hit or chase! But, I decided I would ride on the stationary bicycle for twenty minutes a day, in addition to working the weight machines. The first day I was bored after about five minutes on the bike and thought about quitting. But then I decided I would do it for ten minutes that first day. The second day I got back on the bike and again was bored after five minutes. However, I was determined to continue for at least the same ten minutes as the first day; then I decided I would go longer than I had the first day, and so I continued for two extra minutes. The third day I again extended the time on the bicycle, eventually reaching my goal of twenty minutes. What had happened? I had set small, achievable goals for myself to help me achieve my primary goal.

Lee Iacocca used to go into his home office each Sunday evening and write out his goals for the coming week. These were short-term goals. The path to success requires the discipline to pick up one foot at a time and place it in front of the other. Businesses regularly have three- or even five-year strategic plans. They have annual goals and intermediate strategies for achieving those goals. We need that type of disciplined structure in everything we do.

We all know of the instant gratification that defines much of our world today. We want it and we want it now! But nothing that is really valuable can be achieved in an instant. It is always the result of sustained effort over a long period of time, often with serious setbacks along the way. Many of us set unrealistic goals for ourselves and then are tempted to quit when we can't achieve them. The most important rule for continued success is to set easily achievable intermediate goals for ourselves so that we have a sense of success every day.

I don't think it makes sense to strive for perfection. Perfection is not attainable. I totally believe in striving for excellence, and I think there is a great deal of difference between the two. Although we strive for excellence, we set sensible goals because one of the most frustrating things in the world is to set our goals so high that we have no chance of meeting them.

— Bart Starr, Hall of Fame quarterback

When I was younger and a competitive tennis player, I remember learning a lesson from a great player. He said, "Do something with every shot." In other words, don't think about winning games or even points; play the shot you have, focus on it, and do something with it. If you're behind 0-40, or ahead 40-0, play the shot and give it your best effort. We often hear golfers espouse the same truth: Play the shot you have. It's the only shot we have control over. Playing it as well as we can is the short-term goal.

SETTING GOALS IS LINKED TO OUR SELF-IMAGE

One of the reasons that we set goals for ourselves is out of personal pride. We may set daily goals, weekly goals, monthly goals, or seasonal goals. Whenever we set a goal, it should be something that challenges us but at the same time is achievable. When we work hard at anything, we have the satisfaction of what we have done, whether it is raking a yard, writing a paper, or learning to dribble. Our personal pride is not a reflection of how good our work is compared with that of others (the paper may not be the best in the class, we may not be the best dribbler on the team), but it's a reflection of the progress and effort we have made. It is vitally important to our own senses of self that each of us not settle for the lackadaisical. When we do that, we cannot hold our heads up, because we know we have betrayed ourselves by not giving our best effort.

SETTING GOALS IS PART OF OUR RESPONSIBILITY AS TEAMMATES

Another reason we set goals for ourselves is out of respect for our team. When we join a team, we are making a commitment to our teammates. This is not necessarily acknowledged, but it should be understood. This is why it is important for everyone to be on time for practice, to encourage one another, and to take responsibility for our time with the team. The team commits to doing its best to win. In order for the team to reach its full potential, each member must work to achieve his or her full potential. If a person misses practice or shows up late, the team suffers. Equally, if a person makes little or no effort to improve, the team suffers.

SETTING GOALS IS A REFLECTION ON THOSE WE REPRESENT

We set goals for ourselves while also knowing that we will create a positive image for those we represent: our coach, our family, our team. We are judged by those who are our teammates, family, friends, and even by those we do not know who watch us as we practice and play. Our reputation, and that of those we represent, is established by the character we exhibit day in and day out, in practice and in games.

HOW TO SET AND ACHIEVE OUR GOALS

We are all familiar with setting goals. First, we establish a long-term goal. Then, we establish objectives. Then, we determine a work plan for each objective. This is easier said than done, but determination to create a detailed plan is essential to long-term success.

THE SECRET TO SUCCESS: ABW'S "RULE OF THREES"

What I call the Rule of Threes is the concept that when we choose a goal, we try to have three objectives, three action items for each objective, and three bite-size pieces for each action item. Now, it is hard to create that much detail sometimes, but the more detail we create, the easier it is to follow our "game plan."

THE BIG "MO"

We all know about the big "Mo" (momentum) and that's what success is built on, one small success after another. The secret is to create enough small successes so that every day we are accomplishing at least one thing. It's like going on a diet—if we've lost some weight every time we get on the scale, we'll keep on trying. Similarly, if we have met achievable tasks each day, we will want to keep on succeeding.

The key to success is the positive energy that you generate by breaking your goal down into smaller steps, because the only way anyone ever gets anywhere is one step at a time. The secret is in the energy that comes from doing those bite-size pieces.

Here's what it might look like if we wanted to base creating a goal on one of the tenets:

Goal: I will be a positive influence on the other relationships on the team.

Objective 1: Overcome personal issues between two players.

Action item 1: Choose two players who have personal issues between them.

Bite-size pieces:

- Get to know each player individually.
- Invite both of them to do something with you socially.
- Find another teammate to do the same things.

Action item 2: Choose a social event just for the team: bowling, movie, party.

Bite-size pieces:

- Determine the time and place.
- Make sure everyone is coming.
- Create some funny prizes.

Action item 3: Be positive in practices.

Bite-size pieces:

- Be verbally encouraging and supportive.
- Ask others for opinions and advice.
- Be early, eager, and stay late whenever possible.

Objective 2: Get to know as many of my teammates as possible.

Action item 1: Get together with teammates individually.

Bite-size pieces:

- Choose those you know least first.
- Ask about their backgrounds, interests, etc.
- Share some personal things about yourself.

Action item 2: Be proactive outside of practice.

Bite-size pieces:

- Use locker-room time to talk to others.
- Make an effort to speak to others in class, hall, etc.
- Look for reasons to make a follow-up phone call.

Action item 3: Generate a team service project.

Bite-size pieces:

- Talk to others about ideas; solicit suggestions.
- Encourage others to take leadership.
- Celebrate afterward and compliment all.

Objective 3: This might be to repeat Objective 1 with a different two players, or you might wish to stop with only two objectives.

I know what you're saying!
"My team is too big; I can't do this for everyone."
No, but you can for some.
"Ok. I've got the idea, but I don't really need to do all this detailed planning. I get the idea. I'll do it."
But you've known it before and haven't done it.

PLAYBOOK EXERCISE

- When was the last time you set goals for yourself?
- What is the difference between goal setting and a "to-do list?"
- Would you be willing to set goals with a peer and review them regularly?
- Do you have a sense of pride because you are moving in a clear direction?
- What does it mean in your life to "do something with every shot?"

NEXT STEPS

- Goals: Choose a goal that is achievable within thirty to sixty days.
- Prioritize: Determine how much time you will spend each day working toward that goal. Make sure it is a number you can achieve. It's better to commit to thirty minutes a day and succeed than to commit to sixty minutes and only do forty-five. You will find energy in succeeding and lose energy in failing.
- Objectives: Choose your three objectives.
- Bite-size pieces: Make sure they are easily achievable.

"... AND GIVE MY BEST EFFORT IN PRACTICE AND COMPETITION."

2.3 WORK ETHIC

There are few things more American than what we call "the Protestant work ethic." That work ethic is perhaps best symbolized by the Puritans, hearty Calvinists who first came to the shores of this country believing in hard work, sacrifice, and a serious and uncompromising view of life. For these people work was a duty that deserved their highest priority, gave meaning to life, and contributed to the moral worth of the individual as well as to the health of the social order. Additionally, inherent within the Protestant work ethic is the assumption that usually a person finds success and wealth not because that person is smarter than another, but rather because he or she works harder than the other. These values, imported from Europe, came into the American psyche so completely that they are seen as "American" values. For this reason, hard work, discipline, and sacrifice are among the first things associated with success and the American spirit.

> Whether you think you can or think you can't, you're right.
> — Henry Ford

Each of us must develop personal pride and respect for ourselves so that we will not cheat ourselves by giving only a half effort, by being satisfied with the sloppy, the inadequate, or anything less than our best.

But how do we do that? How do we make ourselves do the things we do not want to do? The determination to give our best effort requires tremendous self-discipline. It is always easy to quit after we have made a solid effort in practice and have become tired, or we tried hard for three-fourths of a game and now find our team well behind. The will to persevere is not different from any other skill. It requires intentional behavior: to give our best effort no matter what. And that decision must be chosen and repeated every day so it becomes a habit.

I remember as a high school soccer player that at the end of practice we ran wind sprints. I also remember that after the wind sprints were over and practice was over, most of the team walked back to the locker room, but some of us ran all the way in, a distance of about 500 yards. That extra 500 yards reflected our desire to give our best effort in practice. We did not want to play in a game for which we were not in the best possible physical condition, and so we pushed ourselves. There is no worse feeling in any game than the feeling that your opponent is more energized than you are. There is no worse feeling than when someone else comes out ahead of you only because he or she has prepared more and worked harder. The same is true in every aspect of life.

One of the things my father used to emphasize was "five extra minutes." He said that, in any endeavor, if I would give an extra five minutes after I thought I was finished, the result would be remarkable. Giving five extra minutes is a matter of will, of the will to go the extra mile, and it applies to anything we do in life.

> You hit home runs not by chance, but by preparation.
> — Roger Maris

When I was in high school my grandfather gave me a poem that he had clipped out of a U.S. Army newspaper when he was in Camp Sevier, South Carolina, in 1917. I have carried it with me because it speaks volumes about the importance of self-discipline and focus in our efforts.

OVER THE PLATE
by
Grantland Rice

> Bill Jones had the speed of a cannon ball;
> He could loosen a brick from a three-foot wall;
> When he shot one across it would hurtle by
> Too swift for even the surest eye.
> No one could hit him when he was right,
> As no eye could follow, the ball's swift flight.
> Bill should have starred in a Big League role,
> But he stuck to the minors, he lacked control.

Jack Smith had the curves of a loop-the-loop,
It would start for your head with a sudden swoop
And break to your knees with a zig-zag wave.
And the league's best hitters would roar and rave
At the jump it took and the sudden swerve.
Shades of a boomerang, what a curve!
But Jack's doomed to a Bush League fate,
He could not get it over the plate.

Tom Brown had both the speed and the curves,
A combination that jarred the nerves.
He would steam 'em by till they looked like peas.
They would take a break from your neck to your knees.
From the best to the worst in the league, by jing!
He had 'em all in the phantom swing.
But he missed the mark of a truly great,
Poor Tom, he couldn't locate the plate.

How is it with you, if I may ask,
Have you got control of your daily task?
Have you got control of your appetite,
Of your temper and tongue in the bitter fight?
Have you got control of your brawn and brain,
Or are you laboring all in vain?
It matters not what your daily role,
Have you got control, have you got control?

It matters not what you "may have" my friend,
When the story is told at the game's far end.
The greatest brawn and the greatest brain
The world has known may be yours in vain.
The one with control is the one who mounts,
And it's how you use what you've got that counts.
Have you got the beam, are you aiming straight?
How much of your effort goes over the plate?

PLAYBOOK EXERCISE

- How would others describe your work ethic?
- How would you describe your own sense of pride in your efforts?
- Which lines in Rice's poem are the most meaningful to you?

NEXT STEPS

- Memorize the last two verses (16 lines) of the poem.
- Determine one way that you will spend five extra minutes each day after you think you are finished.

2.4 SELF-DISCIPLINE

Nothing will work unless you do.
— John Wooden

Each of us has known a person who worked harder than others. Each of us has seen how those who make that extra effort discover the extra dividend. Each of us has, at one time or another, taken a few more minutes each day to make something better than it would have been otherwise.

Practice requires self-discipline. Most athletes do not enjoy the drudgery of repeating the same aspect of their sport. Golfers do not want to practice the same three-foot putt for hours on end; basketball players do not want to practice the same shot over and over again, and few enjoy the rigors of conditioning. Self-discipline, grounded in the desire to excel to the best of our ability, leads us to continue to do what is best for our development, not what is most fun. The hardest part of growing up is learning that we have to do some things we do not want to do. The degree to which we are successful in that effort is usually the degree to which we are successful in whatever we are undertaking.

The hardest part of growing up is learning that we have to do some things we do not want to do.

Many people have trouble asking for the advice and help of others. But one of the surest ways to improve is by asking others—a coach, boss, teammates, or peers—the ways they feel we could improve. We all know that it takes a big person to ask for help, but part of becoming a better person is by being a bigger person.

Nothing is more challenging than having the self-discipline to give our best effort in competition no matter what the score. One day while I was writing this chapter, the Atlanta Braves were ahead 10-1 but went on to lose the baseball game to the Colorado Rockies 12-10. How easy it would have been for the Rockies to have given up!

The opening of a famous graduation speech by Winston Churchill was "Never give in. Never give in. Never, never, never, never —in nothing, great or small, large or petty—never give in, except to convictions of honor and good sense."

The phrase "never give in" is often quoted by others, but Churchill made it famous. It requires a special discipline to continue to give our best effort no matter the score. This is true in so many and varied ways in life. Whether we are attempting to raise a child, train a new employee, learn a new software program, build a new business, or launch a new product, it takes determination to continue when you are the only one who will know the effort you have made.

Never give in. Never give in. Never. Never. Never. Never-
— The opening of Winston Churchill's graduation speech at his old school, Harrow

The same is true for our efforts in practice or in games. Consider either basketball or soccer, for example. In both of these games, the action is often on the other side of the court or field, and we are tempted to rest, catch our breath, and watch what is happening. But great players work just as hard "away from the ball." This means getting into position for a rebound, to be ready for a pass, or to defend. It requires the extra effort that means giving our best effort.

But this is not easy or automatic. Kipling writes that you are growing up "If you can force your heart and nerve and sinew ...to hold on when there is nothing in you except the Will..." You have to "force" yourself to persevere; it is an act of sheer will. But such acts of will are not something that can be turned on like a switch. This is a mistake many athletes make: believing that when it is crunch time they will be able to make that special effort. In fact, this is another example of the truth of the old saying, "you play as you practice." If we do not make the extra effort as a part of our routine, we will not have the resources to do so when it matters. The truth is that the will to put in extra effort is a skill to be developed and strengthened like any other.

> If you can force your heart and nerve and sinew
> To serve your turn long after they are gone,
> And so hold on when there is nothing in you
> Except the Will which says to them: 'Hold on!'
> — Rudyard Kipling

PLAYBOOK EXERCISE

- List the areas in which you are well-disciplined.
- List the areas in which you are less well-disciplined.
- What are some positive examples of when you have been most determined to succeed?
- When have you failed? Why?
- What would working "away from the ball" mean in your life?

NEXT STEPS

- Set as a goal either to be more disciplined or to strengthen your will to excel.
- Determine your objectives, action items, and bite-size pieces to succeed in your goal.

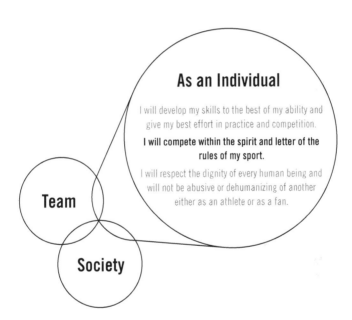

Living The Code as an Individual

As an Individual

I will develop my skills to the best of my ability and give my best effort in practice and competition.

I will compete within the spirit and letter of the rules of my sport.

I will respect the dignity of every human being and will not be abusive or dehumanizing of another either as an athlete or as a fan.

Team

Society

THE SECOND TENET

In Chapter 3, we will examine the place of rules in our lives and in sports, and then break down the two elements of this tenet, "the spirit" and "the letter," and discuss how they are at the foundation of our lives.

The chapter is organized this way:

"I will compete within...the rules of my sport."
3.1 Thinking About Rules
3.2 Rules: The Heart of Every Game

"I will compete within...the letter of the rules..."
3.3 Truth and Honesty

"I will compete within the spirit...of the rules..."
3.4 Integrity and Honor
3.5 Courage

"I WILL COMPETE WITHIN...THE RULES OF MY SPORT."

3.1 THINKING ABOUT RULES

On his 45th birthday, Argentinian professional golfer Roberto De Vicenzo had just completed his greatest tournament. With a final round of 65 he had won the 1968 Masters golf tournament. He went into the scorer's tent to sign his scorecard, which, as is the custom in golf, had been filled out by his playing partner. His signature would certify that it was correct. He signed it and came out to celebrate his win. But, as it turned out, his playing partner had put down an incorrect score on the next-to-last hole, and so, according to the rules of golf, De Vicenzo lost the tournament. The fact that everyone, including a national television audience, knew that he had made a par not a bogey on that hole, did not change the plain language of Rule 6-6. De Vicenzo did not say, "I should be given another chance to correct the scorecard," or "This is a silly rule." Instead, in his broken English, he said, "What a stupid I am to be wrong here."

Now, imagine yourself standing downtown on a freezing street corner in the middle of February at 3 in the morning, with no cars in sight in any direction. The thermometer is at freezing and the wind is blowing hard, making the air feel 20 degrees colder. You need to cross the street to get to your parked car, but the pedestrian light is blinking "Don't Walk." There is nothing moving in any direction. Not a car in sight. Do you wait for the light? Or do you go ahead and cross the street?

There is something about the word "rules" that conjures up negative feelings within us. This is because rules limit our freedom. If there were no rules, we could do anything we wanted, anytime we wanted to do it.

As children, we long to grow up because then there won't be any grown-ups to tell us what to do. We'll be free! And yet, as we grow up, we learn that rules are necessary for every aspect of life, because they provide order and structure to things. Without rules (such as laws), life would be chaotic. I have given children a ball and told them to play a game, but, of course, they cannot play any game until they decide what the rules will be. Equally, you can tell a group of children playing basketball or soccer (or any sport) to play with "no rules," and they rejoice, but it only takes a minute for them to stop and want to resume again with the rules back in place. Without rules, there can be no game, no fun.

PLAYBOOK EXERCISE

- Would you cross the street?
- What feelings (not thoughts) do you have when you hear the word "rules?"
- What thoughts do you have?
- Do you know any rules that seem to serve no purpose?

NEXT STEPS

- Determine the place of rules in your life.
- Write down the two or three most valuable personal rules by which you live. What is their purpose?

3.2 RULES: THE HEART OF EVERY GAME

A baseball umpire was once asked about the challenge and difficulty of calling pitches that were right on the line between being balls or strikes. How did he do it? "Well," he said, "there are balls and there are strikes, but they're nothing until I call them!" With baseball pitches, it is the umpire who interprets the rules of play.

It is important to acknowledge the positive value that rules provide, because they are often viewed as a necessary evil rather than the heart of the game. The truth is that it is the rules that make every game possible, as well as every great play or point in the game. Rules limit what we can do and thus provide the challenge to win a point or a game despite the difficulties thereby imposed. In other words, it is the rules of any game that not only define the game but constitute the heart and soul of the game, and so to attack the rules is to attack the game itself. Equally, the more we seek to honor and live by the rules, the more respect and honor we demonstrate for the game itself.

> It is the rules of any game that constitute the heart and soul of the game, and so to attack the rules is to attack the game itself.

You may not think of it at the outset, but the way we approach the rules of a game is a direct reflection of ourselves, of the values and principles we hold. When we talk about "playing by the rules" we are not really talking about an incident here or there; we are talking about who we are at our core. Are we truthful and honorable, or are we something less than that? Do we respect the game itself above all else, or do we see ourselves as more important, with how we perform and whether we win as more important than the integrity of the game itself?

> When we talk about "playing by the rules" we are not really talking about an incident here or there; we are talking about who we are at our core. Are we truthful and honorable, or are we something less than that?

PLAYBOOK EXERCISE

- Why do you think that the rules of a sport could be thought of as being its soul?
- How does breaking the rules diminish the game itself?
- Who are the people you know who break the rules regularly?

NEXT STEPS

- Think about the love you have for your sport.
- Write down the main thoughts you have about why you love your sport.

- Determine one or more ways you can reflect that love through respect for your sport's rules.

"I WILL COMPETE WITHIN THE … LETTER OF THE RULES…"

3.3 TRUTH AND HONESTY

Derek Jeter of the New York Yankees was at the plate. It was an inside pitch. He spun away to avoid getting hit, and the ball nicked the bat and ricocheted away. As he came to a stop, he immediately grabbed his arm and began jumping around as if he had been hit by the pitch. Since he appeared in apparent great pain, the trainer came out to check his condition. He was awarded first base for being hit by a pitch. Jeter had fooled the umpire. Jeter is regarded as a good sport and a person of integrity, so this incident is a black mark against his name.

The way we follow the rules expresses a direct reflection of ourselves, just as the branches and the fruit of a tree reflect the health of the tree. A tree cannot produce fruit if it is unhealthy or rotten in its core. So it is with us. Telling the truth, playing with honesty and integrity is the sap that feeds our inner being. Living the truth is the fruit that others see.

This is why it is important to develop our core character at every opportunity and to recognize how "who we are" is reflected in countless ways, both on and off the field. The converse is also true. When we encounter those whose fruit is bad—that is, those who seek to skirt or flaunt the rules—we form negative opinions of them. Just as we would not respect a doctor who cheated in medical school, we lose respect for those (including ourselves) who do not play by the rules.

According to legend, George Washington was given a new axe as a boy. When his father asked him if it was he who had chopped down a cherry tree, little Washington famously said, "I cannot tell a lie; I chopped down the tree." This is one of the most well-known anecdotes in American history because it reflects the honest and honorable heart of Washington's character. It was later, as president, that Washington said, "I hope I shall possess firmness and virtue enough to maintain what I consider the most enviable of all titles, the character of an honest man."

> I hope I shall possess firmness and virtue enough to maintain what I consider the most enviable of all titles, the character of an honest man.
>
> — George Washington

President Washington understood that having the character of an honest person required firmness and virtue. He chose firmness because he knew that he would be pulled by peer pressure to "get along by going along," or, in the context of this chapter, to skirt the rules. There is evidently nothing new about people being besieged to compromise their principles, to be asked to support an idea or a person contrary to their beliefs.

When John Wooden was coaching at UCLA and the game was clearly won, it was not uncommon for him to call a timeout, and he did it for two reasons. First, to remind his team that the other team might let their frustration get the better of them, and not to respond or retaliate in any way for things that happened on the floor. And second, to remind them not to celebrate after the game in any way that would offend the other team or their fans. Wooden knew there were always the temptations to respond to the behavior of others, and to gloat over a particularly difficult win. It required firmness and virtue to maintain the proper behavior.

There is an old school prayer that reflects this challenge. It begins as follows:

O God, give me clean hands, clean words, and clean thoughts. Help me to stand for the hard right against the easy wrong. Teach me to work as hard and play as fairly in thy sight alone as if all the world saw.

"Clean" hands, words, thoughts—how much is said in that one sentence! When President Washington said he hoped to have virtue, he meant that he hoped that his innermost being would be clean, filled with the highest moral standard, and that he would remain faithful to that standard. "To stand for the hard right against the easy wrong" is a phrase that needs no explanation; it describes the dilemma we face in countless ways all our lives.

PLAYBOOK EXERCISE

- Do you think the story of George Washington and the cherry tree is historically true? Does it matter?
- Do you think your friends would say you have the firmness that Washington hoped for, to stand for the "hard right?"
- When you hear "to stand for the hard right against the easy wrong," what comes to mind in your experience?

NEXT STEPS

- Determine an issue on which you have been silent and about which you would like to stand for the "hard right." Develop a strategy for how you will do that.
- What is the next step you need to take to make yourself more "clean" than you are now? How will you do it?

"I WILL COMPETE WITHIN THE SPIRIT...OF THE RULES..."

3.4 INTEGRITY AND HONOR

In his prime, Gary Player was regarded as the finest sand player in golf. He was asked how he did it. His answer was that as a young player he would practice hitting out of sand traps until he had made five or until it got dark. Like any of our athletic skills, integrity and honor are not traits that we are born with; they are pillars of our character that are nurtured and developed through rigorous practice day after day.

There is the old expression, "You are what you eat." And it can also be said that you become what you practice. Manners, decency, and moral worth are not things that can be turned on like a faucet; they are habits that are ingrained through repetition. As part of a French play, one of the characters, in speaking about the decline in honorable behavior, says, "I remember when the hungriest man was the last one to lift his fork." That reflection is of behavior that could only have come as the result of a principle ingrained within the person.

We know the discipline required to excel in the physical fundamentals of our sport, but how many of us spend as much time developing our inner character? How often do we see an athlete in a close game "lose it" momentarily? It may come because an opponent has been playing dirty or taunting, and the victim finally snaps, costing the team because of a resulting penalty. Or, who of us has not seen a game in which a player retaliates out of frustration to an action of an opponent, only to be caught in the retaliation and receive a major penalty? It takes far more discipline and strength of character not to respond than to respond.

William Shakespeare's *Hamlet* articulated the importance of maintaining the integrity of our being through Polonius' well-known words to his son:

> "This above all: to thine own self be true, And it must follow, as the night the day, Thou canst not then be false to any man."

To thine own self be true. To be true to yourself means not to betray or compromise your own sense of self, of who you are, of who you want to be and become. Just as President Washington knew that strength of character required firmness, so Shakespeare knew that we are tempted to play different roles in different circumstances. If we act one way with our grandmother, another way with our friends, and still another way elsewhere, who are we? Our life becomes a series of roles, and we have no defined self, no self to whom we are true.

If we act one way with our grandmother, another way with our friends, and still another way elsewhere, who are we?

A businessman once told me about a person he was considering hiring. While they were eating dinner after the interview, the man bragged about a way that he had made a good deal by not being completely honest with the person with whom he was dealing. My friend said simply: "I didn't hire him; if he would act less than honorably in one situation, how could I trust him in my business?"

The businessman knew that people are consistent. If they are honorable in one way, they will be honorable in another; if they are less than honorable in another, they will reflect that same behavior in other ways as well.

Eddie Haskel was a character in the old television series, "Leave It to Beaver." Eddie was a classic example of a "two-faced" person. He would always arrive on the scene smiling, speak to the mother politely, "Good afternoon, Mrs. Cleaver. It is nice to see you. How are you today?" After her response, he would follow it up, still smiling, with a compliment, such as "You certainly do look nice today, Mrs. Cleaver," and continue on his way. Two seconds later, out of her hearing range, his expression would completely change and he would say something like, "What's that jerk Joey doing?" His hypocrisy was what made him amusing to viewers. Unfortunately, we saw something of ourselves in him.

The way we play the game reflects our true inner character. It is not uncommon for young tennis players to call close shots "out." In golf, beginning players routinely improve the lie of their ball, contrary to the rules. What we learn as we grow older is that we cheat ourselves in cheating the game because we compromise on our own sense of self. We are not true to ourselves or to the integrity of our sport.

Who of us has not competed against a person who broke the rules often or who played "dirty?" We have little respect for such a person, and yet that person may not realize the impact his or her behavior has on others. When we realize that cheating or playing dirty reflects on us and on what others think of us, it should make us more determined to play with honor.

We also have competed against people who play cleanly, even in the face of adversity or poor sportsmanship by another. Such people routinely apologize if they unintentionally violate an opponent or make an egregious mistake.

Equally, I can remember in tennis matches seeing an umpire make a bad call, and then the player who was the beneficiary of the bad call deliberately hitting the next ball "out" so as to even the score and not take advantage of the official's mistake. A famous example of this was when Andy Roddick was playing in the 2005 Rome Masters. He was ahead 5-3, 40-0; it was triple match point. His opponent Fernando Verdasco double-faulted, apparently giving the match to Roddick. Roddick, however, protested that the serve was good. The umpire reversed himself, giving the point to Verdasco, who then proceeded to come back to win the game and the match.

The most important reason to play by the spirit of the rules is because it is only when one has won the contest fairly that there is any real sense of accomplishment. A hollow feeling comes from knowing that the score does not tell the truth.

Cal Ripken Jr. tells the story of an occasion when someone tried to do the "hidden ball" trick on an opponent (when a baseball player pretends to throw the ball back to the pitcher but keeps it, hoping that the base runner will step off the bag so he can tag out the duped runner). Ripken said, "My father said, 'I don't want you ever to try that trick.'" "Why not?" Ripken asked, knowing that it was a favorite of all young players. "Because there is no honor in winning that way. Win by playing by the rules and the way the game is intended to be won."

Our lives should be an outward and visible sign of our inner character. The appeal we are making is that we reflect the spirit and not just the letter of the rule. This is the highest standard.

A wonderful example of this is one of the most memorable scenes of good sportsmanship in recent years. It took place in a women's college softball game. The batter hit a home run but while rounding first base, she somehow injured her ankle so that she could not walk. The rules require that the hitter touch all the bases. Unable to stand, she was picked up by her opposing infielders and literally carried around the bases so that she could touch them, and then they returned her to her dugout. According to the letter of the law, they could have left her on the ground and the umpire would have had to call her out.

A few years ago I heard a judge speaking on the occasion of graduation. He was talking about honor and truth, and about living a life of which a person could be proud. One of the things he said was: "People ask me often if something is 'legal.' That is not the question they should be asking—that is 'bottom fishing,' asking if something is 'legal.' They should be asking themselves, 'Is it right?'"

The judge is talking about the difference between the spirit of the law and the letter of the law, and he was making his appeal for that higher standard.

> **People ask me often if something is 'legal.' That is not the question they should be asking—that is 'bottom fishing,' asking if something is 'legal.' They should be asking themselves, 'Is it right?'**
>
> — A judge in Georgia

Athletes are often tempted to skirt and even break the rules if they think they won't be caught.

There is no question that the notion of personal honor is not regarded in the same way as it has been. Alexander Hamilton was one of the distinguished founders of the country. He became the first secretary of the treasury. Hamilton, however, felt that his honor had been slighted one day by Aaron Burr, and so he participated in a duel, which resulted in his death. We may think that words are never worth a duel to the death, but how many of us would even consider our own sense of honor and integrity that valuable?

In Edmond Rostand's play *Cyrano de Bergerac*, de Bergerac was a proud and tragic figure. The symbol of his personal honor and integrity was a white plume that he wore in his hat. At the end of the play, he is dying and losing his mind, and he cries out these words:

> **"I recognize you—all my old enemies. Lying. Compromise. Prejudice. Cowardice. Silliness. *(He flails his sword wildly in the air.)* Never mind – I'll fight on. You would try to take everything from me, all my glory, but when I enter heaven I'll take one thing with me, without a wrinkle or a spot, and that is, *(gasping for air)* ... that is ... my white plume!"**

No matter what happened to de Bergerac, he had his honor, his sense of his own integrity unspotted by the world. He had succumbed to death, but not to his "old enemies." Will we be able to say that?

Families used to have coats of arms and often Latin mottos that reflected the values most highly prized by the family. The same is true for businesses, cities, states, countries. There are probably no words more commonly used in these mottos than honor, truth, or virtue. They all describe the attributes of the kind of person we most value.

PLAYBOOK EXERCISE

- How often do you think you are "true" to your best self? How often do you play a role that you think others will like?
- Who are examples of friends whose behavior is a reflection of who they are at their core? Who seems to you always to be playing a role?
- Do you agree or disagree with the businessman who thought that if people cheated in one area of their lives they would cheat in others?
- Do you agree with Cal Ripken Jr.'s father's advice? What can be said about both sides of that question?
- Cyrano de Bergerac had his "old enemies," which he named. What would the list of your "enemies" include?
- How would you define "honor?"

NEXT STEPS

- Cal Ripken Jr.'s father's attitude, as well as that of the judge, reflects a high sense of personal integrity. What are the ways that higher sense could be communicated to your team?
- Make a design of a personal coat of arms. It should include at least four symbols. What would your motto be? What symbols would you choose and why?

3.5 COURAGE

One of our sons attended Wake Forest University. While he was there he had the privilege of taking a class with Dr. Maya Angelou, the famous poet and author. One day she asked the class to suggest what they thought was the most important virtue. As they went around the room, different students had different ideas: truthfulness, kindness, compassion, honesty, humility, and so on. When they were all finished, she said, "I think the most important virtue is courage, because without it, you will not act on any of the others consistently."

> ### I think the most important virtue is courage, because without it, you will not act on any of the others consistently.
> — Maya Angelou

Dr. Angelou's answer reflects the same sentiment as Aristotle had. Although Aristotle considered wisdom the greatest virtue, he considered courage as the first virtue, because, he said, it makes all of the other virtues possible. Courage is not something that everyone has in equal amounts. It is, however, like all of the virtues, something that can be nurtured, grown, and developed. When we ask for help to stand for the hard right against the easy wrong, we are asking for courage.

Courage comes in many forms. It takes courage to do something for the first time. It takes courage to trust another person to do something important for you. It takes courage to speak out or to act against the popular thing, to go against the tide of public opinion. It takes courage to act in the face of danger.

Many of us are like the lion in *The Wizard of Oz*. We are nice people who wish we were more courageous. But that is the first step: to admit we wish we were more courageous. Then we have a choice. Shall we become more courageous, or shall we remain as we are?

There are many examples of times when people are less than courageous, when the effort is made to try to fit in, to get along, to not rock the boat. It is important to know that when we are not "true to our self," as Shakespeare said, something within our soul and spirit dies. This is the consequence of not having the courage of our convictions. We lose respect for ourselves, and our own sense of self is damaged.

Many of us are like the lion in The Wizard of Oz. We are nice people who wish we were more courageous.

One of the things we have been repeating is that it takes practice to become better at anything. The same is true for courage. We become more courageous by practicing taking small courageous steps. Let me give an example. First, think of an issue about which you disagree with others but have not told them. It would take courage for you to disagree with those with whom you have pretended to agree. Then, think of how you could express your true feelings to at least one other person. If you do that, you will find that if they are your friend, they may disagree with you, but it will not change your friendship. You will find new life and energy within for having been honest with them and with yourself. Our own inner being is inspired by the positive actions we take, just as it can be damaged by our failure to be true to ourselves. More than anything, as we take the first steps in acting courageously, we find the courage to take the next step.

Playing by the rules represents far more than playing by the rules. Who we are is expressed by how we value and live out the rules—all the rules, all the time. And who we are is far more important than any game.

PLAYBOOK EXERCISE

- Do you agree with Maya Angelou and Aristotle? What are the three virtues you consider the most important?
- Which people you know do you consider "courageous?" In what ways have they shown courage that others have not?
- What is the place of fear in your life? In what areas do you let fear determine your action?

NEXT STEPS

- Choose one area in which you want to find the courage that has been lacking before. Then, have the courage to talk about it with a friend. Are you able to set some achievable goals for yourself?

CHAPTER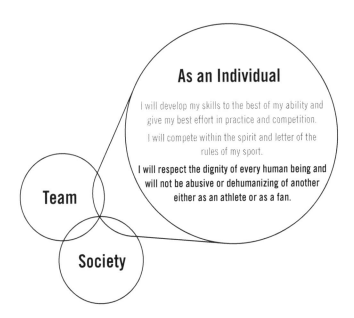

Living The Code as an Individual

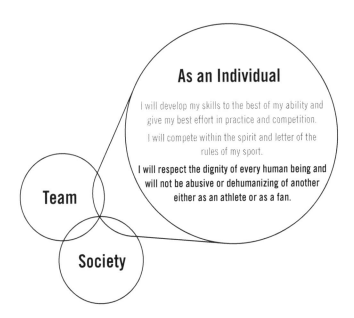

As an Individual

I will develop my skills to the best of my ability and give my best effort in practice and competition.

I will compete within the spirit and letter of the rules of my sport.

I will respect the dignity of every human being and will not be abusive or dehumanizing of another either as an athlete or as a fan.

Team

Society

THE THIRD TENET

In this chapter we will examine our attitude toward others. How do we view those who are different from us? What does it mean to "respect" others? Are we to respect even those whose behavior is contrary to our standards? The chapter is organized in the following way:

"I will respect the dignity of every human being and will not be abusive or dehumanizing of another, either as an athlete or as a fan."

"I will respect the dignity of every human being..."
4.1 The Problem Is Not New
4.2 The Dignity of Every Person
   You Must Respect the Ball
   Stereotyping
4.3 The Barriers to Respecting Dignity
   Racism
   Religious Prejudice
   Demonizing the Opposition
4.4 Removing the Barriers
   Moments of Self-discovery and Understanding
   Moving from Tolerance to Acceptance and Inclusion

"... and will not be abusive or dehumanizing of another, either as an athlete or as a fan."
4.5 Abusive and Dehumanizing Speech
   Booing, Taunting, and Trash Talking
4.6 Developing Self-control
   Before Practice or the Game
   During the Game
   After the Game
4.7 A Final Story

"I WILL RESPECT THE DIGNITY OF EVERY HUMAN BEING..."

4.1 THE PROBLEM IS NOT NEW

Did you know...

...that when Jack Johnson became the heavyweight boxing champion the white community was so upset that boxer Jim Jeffries was dubbed "the Great White Hope?"

...about the negative reaction from some when Sandy Koufax of the Los Angeles Dodgers and Hank Greenberg of the Detroit Tigers refused to play in a World Series game because each game fell on Yom Kippur, the holiest day in the Jewish calendar?

...about the similar reactions when English runner Eric Liddell refused to race in the Olympics because it fell on Sunday?

...that Hitler wanted to use the 1936 Olympics in Berlin as an opportunity to showcase Aryan superiority—until the African-American Jesse Owens won four gold medals?

...that as a coach in Indiana John Wooden refused to let his team compete against a team that had previously refused to compete against another team with African-Americans on it?

The issues of race and racism, of prejudice and intolerance, have all found their challenges expressed in the world of sports. So too have sports been one of the vehicles for human growth and progress. Sports have played a major role in the transformation of individuals and society.

4.2 THE DIGNITY OF EVERY PERSON

YOU MUST RESPECT THE BALL

Pierre Etchebaster was arguably the greatest champion of any sport in history. He was the world champion of court tennis for 26 years, defeating every challenger who came his way and dominating his sport for over two generations—a claim no other champion can make in any sport! Court tennis is the original racquet game, played indoors over a net but with walls, windows, and a roof also in play. I had the good fortune to take a lesson from Etchebaster when he was in his 80s but still active. One of the things he said to me has stayed with me: "You must respect the ball." It had never occurred to me that I should "respect" a tennis ball! I've thought about it often. Every ball is similar on the one hand, but on the other hand, as it reaches me, it has its own speed, spin, and angle, and so it has its own personality. I cannot treat each ball as if it is like every other ball that comes my way. I must respect and value the uniqueness of each.

You must respect the ball.
— Pierre Etchebaster

Like a tennis ball, whenever we see others coming toward us we are always pre-judging them—how they look, what they are doing, what they are saying (or not saying). In one sense, we have no control over our judgments and forethoughts; they simply come to us. But as thinking people we are able to rise above our immediate non-thinking reactions with a mature, reasoned response.

No matter who we are, we are likely to assume that people who look like us, dress like us, and talk like us are like us. We are usually comfortable with those who seem to be like us; however, those who are different may register different feelings within us.

What do we mean when we say we will respect the dignity of every human being? The word "dignity" is the key. It comes from the Latin word *dignus*, which means "worth." Each person has worth. Every person has value.

When the founders wrote that all men are created equal, they did not mean that all people have equal brains, looks, athletic abilities, or anything like that. They meant simply and profoundly, as Albert Schweitzer said, that "the other person is a person, just as I am." We all have the same inherent worth. No one is more of a person than anyone else. Some may be more "valuable" to society (a medical doctor or a teacher, for example), some may be more valuable to our government (a soldier or politician, for example), some of us may be more valuable to business (a banker or client, for example), and still others may be more valuable to the continued life of society (a farmer, for example).

> ## The other person is a person, just as I am.
> — Albert Schweitzer

STEREOTYPING

One of the interesting value-clarification games to play is called "Fall-out shelter." This is the way the game works: Only five people can fit into the shelter. A nuclear bomb is on its way. Which five of the following ten people get to enter? 1. Male bookkeeper, thirty-one years old; 2. His wife, six months pregnant; 3. Male Third World radical, second-year medical student; 4. Famous male historical author, forty-two years old; 5. Hollywood actress/singer/dancer; 6. Male biochemist; 7. Rabbi, fifty-four years old; 8.Male Olympic athlete, all sports; 9. Female student; 10. Male policeman with gun (cannot be separated)

The purpose of this game is to reveal to us the prejudices we have. Do they lie with age, nationality, religion, profession, sexuality, or something else?

Since there is a temptation to think that some people are more valuable than others, this can easily lead to the idea that we don't need some people; that we would be better off without some people; people whose activities are so bad in our view that they should be done away with. This can lead to the notion that some people are worth more than others, that some people are superior to others, and that others are expendable. How do we overcome the temptation to see others as less than ourselves?

PLAYBOOK EXERCISE

- When you see a person you don't know, what are some of the assumptions you make? Where do those stereotypes come from?

- What do "dignity" and "worth" mean to you for a person who dresses differently, speaks a different language, or comes from a different country?
- Are there some people you don't like? Do you see yourself as in some sense better than they are? What would they say about you?
- In what ways can someone say that there is a dignity or worth to every human being, no matter how badly they may behave?
- How can you show respect for a person whose behavior you find reprehensible?
- How do we learn from those who differ most from us?

NEXT STEPS

- What are the ways you can show respect for a person whose values you reject?
- Identify at least one individual or group that you think is unfairly judged by others.
- Determine at least one way you are now going to act differently toward another person. What steps do you have to take to see the other person as having worth?

4.3 THE BARRIERS TO RESPECTING DIGNITY

RACISM

I grew up in Asheville, North Carolina. Since I was born in 1945, I became aware of my surroundings in the late '40s and early '50s. At that time, segregation was a way of life in the South. Blacks and whites lived in two separate worlds: separate places to live, eat, or sit on the bus; separate waiting rooms in bus or train stations; separate areas in theatres, usually blacks in the balcony. The black person had been defined in the U.S. Constitution as two-thirds of a person, and two hundred years later they were still not considered whole people in the eyes of many white people. The blacks were in some way inferior. This was the world order into which I was born, and it did not occur to me that anything was wrong. The black person was valued but valued less than the white neighbor.

RELIGIOUS PREJUDICE

When I was in the eighth grade we moved to Massachusetts and lived in a house in the country. A Jewish family, who had a son my age named Marc, lived across the street. He and I became best friends. At the time, I had never met a Jewish person and knew nothing about Jews, except that they were a different religion. It was at that same time that Jack Kennedy, our senator, ran for president. Some people made issue of his being a Catholic, just another faith as far as I knew (I was a protestant Episcopalian). Within a few months, however, I learned that some people had very negative opinions about both Catholics and Jews. The song from *South Pacific* seemed to have a message:

> You've got to be taught to hate and fear
> You've got to be taught from year to year
> It's got to be drummed in your dear little ear,
> You've got to be carefully taught.
> You've got to be taught before it's too late
> Before you are six or seven or eight
> To hate all the people your relatives hate
> You've got to be carefully taught.

DEMONIZING THE OPPOSITION

In war, each side will demonize the other. This is done to remove the humanity from the other side, to make it easier to hate them, and, ultimately, to kill them without feeling remorse or guilt. In the Second

World War, Japan was vilified as the "Yellow Peril." More recently, Ronald Reagan famously referred to Russia as the "Evil Empire." In demonizing the opposition, we remove their humanity. Unfortunately, this is also a practice that goes on frequently in peacetime, most commonly in politics and sports. Sports fans like to demonize the opposition. Big cities like New York, Boston, Philadelphia, Los Angeles, and Chicago are often demonized by many in other cities, most of whom do not know a single person in the other city! High school sports teams and their fans will consider their rival high school's team and its fans to be barbaric, classless, ignorant, dirty, or simply people of no worth.

PLAYBOOK EXERCISE

- What are the attitudes you have for those people who are different from you?
- How would you describe the barriers you face in your relationships with others?
- How would you describe your views of those whose religious beliefs are different from yours?
- In what ways do you tend to pre-judge others by their race, religion, or ethnic group?
- Make a list of people you know who are of a different race, religion, or nationality from you. Does knowing these people affect your opinions about their group?
- Why do we "demonize" others?

NEXT STEPS

- Have an open conversation with someone you know whose religion or national origin is different from yours. Ask them how they understand their faith, or why it makes sense to them.
- Do the same with someone from another country. Learn what they value about their homeland and what values they appreciate most here.

4.4 REMOVING THE BARRIERS: SEEING THE OTHER PERSON AS MYSELF

MOMENTS OF SELF-DISCOVERY AND UNDERSTANDING

One day early in my teenage years I suddenly had the realization that the other person was a person, just as I was. It may well have happened in the spring of my eighth-grade year. It was then that we read Shakespeare's play *The Merchant of Venice*. One of the play's central themes revolves around the Jewish merchant, Shylock, who loans money to Antonio. The stereotype of the Jew being somehow different from non-Jews is brought into sharp focus in Shylock's famous speech:

> "I am a Jew. Hath not a Jew eyes? Hath not a Jew hands, organs, dimensions, senses, affections, passions; fed with the same food, hurt with the same weapons, subject to the same diseases, heal'd by the same means, warm'd and cool'd by the same winter and summer, as a Christian is? If you prick us, do we not bleed? If you tickle us, do we not laugh? If you poison us, do we not die? And if you wrong us, do we not revenge?"

Reading this speech made me realize that Shylock was right. I should never generalize about others as if they were somehow less than I was. Surely others must love their parents, love their children, and have hopes and aspirations for themselves and their loved ones, just as I did! They, too, must rejoice and cry and worry and possess all of the same emotional burdens that others carry. I thought about this over and over again. How could I have ever seen another as less than I was? How could I have been so blind?

> If you prick us, do we not bleed?
>
> — Shylock
> The Merchant of Venice

When Jackie Robinson broke the color barrier in baseball with the Brooklyn Dodgers in 1947, many players opposed to the action. Team captain Pee Wee Reese was even presented with a petition that threatened a boycott if Robinson joined the team, but Reese refused to sign it. Then, as Robinson was being heckled by fans in Cincinnati during the Dodgers' first road trip, Reese put his arm around Robinson's shoulder in a gesture of inclusion and support.

Reese was an eight-time all-star who played with seven pennant winners and one World Series champion in Brooklyn. Carl Erskine, a pitcher on the team, also remembered Reese's role in helping Robinson break the color line in baseball. "Think of the guts that took," he said. "Pee Wee had to go home [to segregated Louisville] and answer to his friends ... I told Jackie later that [Reese's gesture] helped my race more than his."

Joe Black, a former Brooklyn pitcher and one of the first African-Americans in Major League Baseball, said, "Pee Wee helped make my boyhood dream come true to play in the majors, the World Series. When Pee Wee reached out to Jackie, all of us in the Negro League smiled and said it was the first time that a white guy had accepted us." He continued, "When I finally got up to Brooklyn, I went to Pee Wee and said, 'Black people love you. When you touched Jackie, you touched all of us.' With Pee Wee, it was No. 1 on his uniform and No. 1 in our hearts."

PLAYBOOK EXERCISE

- As a child, how did you view people of other races, religions, social and economic backgrounds?
- Think of a person you like now but did not like at first. What was the cause for the change?
- List at least two ways your views in social issues have changed. What was it that led you to change your views?
- Have you ever stood up for someone that others were making fun of as Pee Wee Reese did?

NEXT STEP

- Identify a situation in which you can make a difference by including someone who may have been left out, and work out a strategy for so doing.

MOVING FROM TOLERANCE TO ACCEPTANCE TO INCLUSION

In 1970, when Bear Bryant's University of Alabama football team was crushed 42-21 in Birmingham by the University of Southern California with African-American star Sam "Bam" Cunningham scoring three touchdowns, the stage was set for integration of the team. What Alabama fans didn't yet know was that Bryant had already crossed the color line. Sitting in the stands that day was the university's first black scholarship player, Wilbur Jackson, who watched as Sam Cunningham, in Bear Bryant's words, "did more to integrate Alabama in one afternoon than Martin Luther King Jr. had in years."

> Sam Cunningham did more to integrate Alabama in one afternoon than Martin Luther King Jr. had in years.
> — Paul "Bear" Bryant

Bryant's action was similar to that of Pee Wee Reese. Just as Reese was revered in Brooklyn, so the Bear was revered in Alabama. If he was willing to accept black players on his team, then his fans would become more willing to accept them in their lives. But this was just the first step: the step of tolerance, which we take on the way to respect. Tolerance is a passive word; to say that we will "tolerate" something has the connotation of "endure" or "put up with." Not that we would enjoy something, but that we would allow it to happen or to continue. We tolerate many things: traffic to football games, rainy days, or friends who talk too much.

Tolerance means accepting the right of one person to have the same opportunity as others without necessarily embracing it or understanding it. Tolerance of another is to recognize the "letter" of the law, to use the vocabulary of our earlier tenet, but not necessarily the "spirit" of the law: the acceptance that the other person's worth equals mine. Tolerance, however, leads to the next step on the way to respect: acceptance. Acceptance means that we have internally acknowledged that a situation with which we previously disagreed is legitimate, or acceptable, even though we may not like it. When we accept something as valid, we will no longer try to fight it or stop it.

Inclusion is the final step. This is when we do not simply accept something that we previously rejected, but we actively try to make it a part of our lives. It comes when we have learned that those who are different have many positive qualities that will enhance and enrich our own lives.

"…AND WILL NOT BE ABUSIVE OR DEHUMANIZING OF ANOTHER, EITHER AS AN ATHLETE OR AS A FAN."

4.5 ABUSIVE AND DEHUMANIZING SPEECH

BOOING, TAUNTING, AND TRASH TALKING

Jimmy Piersall was an all-star center fielder for the Boston Red Sox (and other teams later) in the 1950s. There is an iconic photo of him sitting down, knees drawn up to his chest, at the base of the flagpole in center field. The photo was taken during a game; he had been taunted one too many times. Piersall had previously suffered emotional problems, had been hospitalized, and ever after was the subject of every sort of taunt by fans, trying to get him to do something "crazy." It worked that day.

As children, we all learn the rhyme "Sticks and stones may break my bones, but words will never hurt me." Why do we all know this? Because even as small children we begin to call each other names, and we get into fights with our playmates. The urge to attack another person with our tongue begins not long after we first learn to talk!

As we enter the world of sports, we boo the official who makes a call that we either don't like or we think was wrong. We taunt opposing players, hoping to upset them and get them off their game, or simply out of meanness on our part, just as the fans taunted Piersall.

Trash talking, which sometimes begins as friendly banter, often ends up with language that leads to fights or worse.

A couple of generations ago, all such behavior was considered bad manners at a minimum and was universally regarded as bad sportsmanship. Why? Why has the culture changed? The answer is simple. We have lost our sense of values, of civility, of respect for others as a matter of course.

Any form of language that attacks another person is a violation of The Code, because all language that attacks a person shows disrespect for that person. There is a big difference between saying, "Pass the ball!" and "Pass the ball, you idiot!" A big difference between just saying, "He was safe!" or "He was out of bounds!" and adding, "Even a blind person could see that!"

The truth is, when we use inappropriate language, the reason we are doing so is to try to hurt the person. When we trash talk opponents, we are attempting to wound their inner being in a way that will lead them to lose control of themselves in some way.

The Golden Rule ("Do unto others as you would have them do unto you") appears in some form in every major religion. It does so because this should be the fundamental test of how we treat others. We should treat them the way we would like to be treated.

So, what are we to do?

4.6 DEVELOPING SELF-CONTROL

Developing self-control is as important as any part of our character development. It comes from the result of mental discipline. Gaining control of our thoughts and words comes as the result of the same sort of consistent and ongoing work and effort that are necessary to improve our physical skills.

> **Gaining control of our thoughts and words comes as the result of the same sort of consistent and ongoing work and effort that are necessary to improve our physical skills.**

We all know that some people have a short fuse and others seem unflappable no matter what the situation. We are all different. But we all need to work to control our emotions. Everyone knows that the mental game is in many ways as important as the physical game. How do we develop our mental game?

BEFORE PRACTICE OR THE GAME

The first step is to "get our heads straight." This means focusing on how we plan to carry ourselves, what we plan to do, what our personal goals are for ourselves. An important part of this mental preparation is thinking through how we will deal with adversity.

Adversity can mean we are not playing well; adversity can mean the team is not playing well; adversity can mean the coach reacts in a way that we weren't expecting or our teammates say or do things we were not expecting; or it can be poor sportsmanship by our opponents or their fans. How do we react to the unexpected? All of these situations are possible, and that is why it is important to have our heads on straight!

So, what do we do? We need to remind ourselves that we will "respect the dignity of every human being... and not be abusive or dehumanizing..." We need to remind ourselves that *this is what we will do*, no matter what the occasion or what comes up.

DURING THE GAME

Anger needs no definition; it is an emotion that we all know well. It is a powerful feeling that can build up slowly or suddenly erupt. It is so strong that it has the potential to overpower our normal thoughts and behaviors.

Emotions come to us from within. We cannot stop emotion, but we can control our reaction to it. In fact, we have to learn how to control our emotions. It is called growing up.

We have to learn how to control our emotions.
It is called growing up.

Some people learn how to control their emotions in only a few areas of their lives. People who yell at their five-year-old's game official, who are rude to the wait staff in restaurants, or who drive recklessly because other drivers anger them are all some examples of those who still have some growing up to do. Their emotions take control of them, and they act like children.

When we receive bad calls from an official, hear taunts from opposing players or fans, it is natural to react internally. But, externally, how do we act? Do we return the taunt verbally? Do we do we respond in some physical way? Or, do we say and do nothing, ignoring the taunt?

If we have our heads on straight, then we might say to ourselves, "We knew this would happen, and we have already determined how we are going to react. We are not going to let this get to us!" Later, as it continues, we might say to ourselves, "We knew this would continue, and we know how we are going to act." Make no mistake. This is not easy. No matter what we have determined before the game, the reality is often extremely challenging. If you have a runner on third base who gets called out on strikes by the umpire on a pitch that you thought was clearly a ball, it is hard to simply walk away as if nothing happened. If you are playing soccer and get tripped as you are about to take a shot and no call is made by the official, it is hard to play on as if nothing happened. If you are bumped off-stride or held by the defender just as you are about to catch a football, and no call is made, it is hard to control your emotions. But, in these and all circumstances, learning to control our emotions, rather than having them control us, is essential.

Many players, managers, and coaches are well-known for the emotional tirades and on-field antics when upset by what they consider bad officiating. But there is another way to react. When Chris Evert played tennis she was often referred to as the "ice queen," because no matter what happened for good or ill, she never changed expression. We are not suggesting that we all become that stoic in our behaviors, nor that we don't express ourselves to an official when we feel we have a legitimate complaint. Learning to control our emotions does not mean that we lose them or bury them, but it does mean that we learn how to channel them in a way that is constructive.

Some people say, "don't get mad, get even." That is not the thing to do. Instead, learn to channel the anger into positive action so that we play more determined and more focused. The great surprise is that often our refusal to respond to the taunts or behavior of others frustrates them, leading them to greater mistakes. One thing is certain: When we do not respond with anger, we earn the respect of all.

Learning to control our emotions does not mean that we lose them or bury them, but it does mean that we learn how to channel them in a way that is constructive.

AFTER THE GAME

We have all seen people who say things after a game that they regret later, things said in anger or frustration or personal disappointment. Sometimes they are said in victory. Once words are spoken, they cannot be taken back. As children we are sometimes taught to count to ten before saying anything. One of the most difficult things to learn is the discipline necessary to hold our tongues, so as not to say things we later regret. It is better to have "no comment" than the wrong comment!

PLAYBOOK EXERCISE

- In what ways have you demonized another group in your past? Are there groups you demonize now? What about the fans of those teams you often oppose; how do you view them?

NEXT STEP

- Determine how you will act and what you will say when you hear someone using abusive or dehumanizing language.

4.7 A FINAL STORY

In France following the D-Day invasion of Normandy, a young soldier was wounded and died a few days later. There was a French Catholic church nearby, and so a few of his friends asked if they might bury their comrade in the cemetery. "Is he Catholic?" the priest asked. "No, he was the son of Methodist minister," was the reply. "No," said the priest. "The cemetery is for Catholics only. However, you can bury him outside the fence. We own that land as well." So, disappointed, they buried him there, outside the fence. Some months later, when the war had ended, the friends returned to place a headstone over the grave. They assumed it would be easy to find, since they knew where they had buried it and the soil would be different where a hole had been dug. They could not find it. Finally, they went in to see the priest. The priest said, "After you all left, I felt very badly and didn't sleep well. So the next day, when I got here, I moved the fence out to include your friend."

Learning to extend the fences is a life-long job.

CHAPTER 5

Living The Code as a Member of a Team

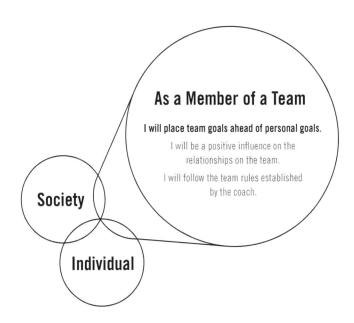

As a Member of a Team

I will place team goals ahead of personal goals.

I will be a positive influence on the relationships on the team.

I will follow the team rules established by the coach.

Society

Individual

THE FIRST TENET

Most sports began with the desire of the individual to play the game. The initial focus is almost always on the individual and his work or her efforts to become in some sense "good." As we begin to play on teams, we have all played with people who were more interested in how they were doing than how the team was doing. This tenet of The Code encourages sacrifice and selflessness instead of selfishness and self-centeredness. It reminds the athlete that the team goal of doing its best (and hopefully winning) is the important goal, not one's own glory, and that it is through cooperation and teamwork that that goal is best accomplished. This chapter is organized as follows:

"I will place team goals ahead of personal goals."

5.1 The Next Step in Character Development
    Sacrifice
    Cooperation
    Reliability
    Team Spirit
5.2 The Challenges
    Egos and Personality Types
    Personality Conflicts
    Injuries and Bad Luck
    Coaching Strategy
5.3 Benefits of Team Play
    Playing as a Team
    The Relationships

5.1 THE NEXT STEP IN CHARACTER DEVELOPMENT

The formation of our character requires the ongoing discipline of the will to reach our higher goals. We have seen that learning to respect others requires us to learn to control the quick impulses of our nature, and to look beyond the superficial characteristics of a person to see that individual as a valued person. We have seen that the development of our skills as an athlete requires us to submit to the daily discipline of drills and exercises in order to lead us to greater proficiency. We have seen that to play the game with honor requires us to develop the mental strength to resist the temptation to cut corners or to look for cheap ways of winning. All character development requires the continual discipline of the will to achieve a higher goal.

When we reflected on the first tenet ("Developing our skills") one of the important considerations was goal setting. We remembered that we will make the most progress if we set clear and achievable goals and work toward them. Developing our skills to the best of our ability requires discipline and work. Each of us must always strive to become the best we are capable of becoming. All personal goals, however, must be placed in the context of the team goals, and the success of the team should always be each player's highest priority.

In coaching, I have often said to my players, "individuals win in individual sports, but teams win in team sports." This is only to make an obvious point: The teams that play the best together, combining the skills of the individuals in a collective whole, are the teams that win. John Wooden always said, "I'd rather have the five players who play best together than the five best players." It is challenging for any coach to best determine the strategy and the methods of having his or her team play as one. One of the joys of coaching is to be successful; to see each person fulfilling a role and becoming a building block of the team.

SACRIFICE

In baseball, if there is a runner on base, the batter will often lay down a bunt so that the runner may move up to the next base. This is called a "sacrifice bunt" because the batter sacrifices himself or herself; that is, the batter makes a deliberate out so a teammate may advance a base. Equally, if a batter hits a fly ball out, which allows a runner to tag up and advance, that is called a "sacrifice fly."

It is interesting that this vocabulary of "sacrifice" has entered into baseball jargon. No ideal is more central to the concept of team play than self-sacrifice. The questions in people's minds are always, What can I do that will make the team better? What can I do that will make this play more cohesive? What can I do that will encourage others to support each other? To be a team player is to think of the team first, to make the success of a team the highest priority. It is to subsume individual interests and personal goals to the larger interests of the team.

> It is interesting that this vocabulary of "sacrifice" has entered into baseball jargon.

John Smoltz, formerly of the Atlanta Braves, was one of the great starting pitchers of this era. Because his team had no effective closer, he was asked if he would be willing to become the closer instead of one of the ace starters. Most pitchers would have been unwilling to even consider such a change. Smoltz, however, was willing to do what was best for the team. In moving to the bullpen, he not only became a feared closer, but remained there for several years before returning as a starter.

PLAYBOOK EXERCISE

- What are some examples in which you have seen players sacrifice for their team?
- List the ways in which you sacrifice for the goals of your team, your family, or others.
- What will you lose by sacrificing for others? What will you gain?

NEXT STEP

- Determine two ways you would next like to make a difference, and what sacrifices that will require of you.

COOPERATION

Teamwork is all about cooperation, and cooperation takes place at several levels.

First, cooperation begins with listening. When the coach or anyone else begins to speak, we cooperate by giving him or her our undivided attention. Communication is vital to any successful program and by cooperating and listening completely and carefully valuable time is saved. Listening shows respect for the person who is speaking and indicates that we value what that person has to say. By listening intently, the goals, strategies, or techniques may be better understood, and possible issues and problems identified. For those who are absent or who do not listen carefully, it will probably mean more time will have to be taken later, to explain again what was missed the first time. The more this occurs, the more the team's progress is delayed.

Second, cooperation includes working with our teammates to internalize and apply the lessons learned. Perhaps we can do something more easily than a teammate. We cooperate by taking the time to help that person understand or practice whatever has been taught. We cooperate by coming out to practice early either to work on our skills or to help a teammate, or by staying late.

Third, we also cooperate when we offer to help out with the little things that make our team stronger. Perhaps it's a willingness to give someone a ride, to carry equipment, to work with a teammate on a particular skill, or to support a teammate who is not playing well.

PLAYBOOK EXERCISE

- How do you see cooperation demonstrated on your team? Are there any barriers to cooperation that you see?
- Identify ways your cooperation could be improved.

NEXT STEP

- Determine a strategy for improving in the areas you identify and a timetable for action.

RELIABILITY

In the opening game of the 1988 World Series, the Oakland Athletics were leading 4-3 going into the bottom of the ninth against the Los Angeles Dodgers. The Dodgers had two outs and a man on first when Kirk Gibson was called on to pinch-hit against Hall of Fame closer Dennis Eckersley. Gibson, who was the heart and soul of the team, as well as its best player, was on the bench because he had a leg injury so severe that he was unable to run. Despite falling behind 0-2 in the count, he worked the count to 3-2 before hitting a home run over the fence in right field to win the game. It was one of the most electric moments in the history of baseball (memorialized by announcer Jack Buck's words "I do not believe what I just saw. Is this really happening, Bill?") and inspired the Dodgers to go on to win the series 4-1. As Gibson limped around the bases, his fist pumps between first and second base were replayed so many times by the media that the fist pump became a part of sports.

> ## "I do not believe what I just saw. Is this really happening, Bill?"
> — Jack Buck

In game five of the 1970 NBA finals, the New York Knicks center Willis Reed was injured and forced to leave the game. He did not play in game six and was assumed to be unable to play in game seven, which Wilt Chamberlain, Jerry West, and the Los Angeles Lakers were expected to win as easily as they had game six. Moments before tip-off, Willis Reed emerged from the locker room. The home crowd went wild in one of the most frenzied moments in the history of basketball. Reed limped onto the floor, dragging his injured leg, and within seconds hit the first shot of the game and then quickly followed with a second basket. He did not score again and was soon on the bench, but his presence inspired his teammates to go on to build up a 29-point lead as they won the game.

Both of these stories tell of incredible moments when an injured player came off the bench to set the tone for the championship. We often hear about playing with pain as a part of sports. Some players are known to play through injuries while others have the reputation of refusing to play if they are not at 100 percent. There are clearly times when it is unwise to play with an injury if one risks exacerbating what might be a minor injury. While we would never condone playing when there is serious risk involved, the willingness to play when suffering some sort of nagging or minor injury reflects a commitment to the team and its goals that take precedence over our own. We all rely on each other to succeed, and our reliability is often tested when we are faced with injuries.

Reliability is not just seen in these dramatic ways. It is most commonly seen in the player who is always on time, if not early. It is the person who goes the extra mile, who never complains, who volunteers, who does things without being asked, whose attitude is always positive, and who supports the team off the field in every possible way.

PLAYBOOK EXERCISE

- Make a list of the three most reliable people you depend on. What are the things they have done that have impressed you?
- Make a list of the times you have felt let down by others.

NEXT STEPS

- Ask your teammates if they think you are reliable.
- Make a list of the small things you can do that will improve your reliability in the eyes of others.

TEAM SPIRIT

In 1979 the Pittsburgh Pirates won the World Series. The team used the theme "we are family," taken from the hit song of that time. On that particular team, players loved and cared for each other as if they were members of the same family; each person would do anything for the other and for the team.

Building team spirit is one of the jobs that comes both with coaching and being a team leader. Developing team spirit requires more than words. Spirit comes from within individuals, and while it cannot be demanded, it can be nurtured. Leadership by the coaching staff and individual players is key to developing team spirit, and that leadership is demonstrated by action more than by words. We respond to what we see more than what we hear. Words are only effective if they have been—and continue to be—reflected by the actions of the person who is speaking.

> **Words are only effective if they have been, and continue to be, reflected by the actions of the person who is speaking.**

One of the important things that we can do is learn about the off-field lives of the team members. Are they good students? What subjects are their best? What other interests do they have? What other sports do they play? Any time coaches or players can be a part of each others' lives off the field, it increases the relationships and helps build team spirit.

It is the quality of the relationships on the team that results in commitment to each other and to the spirit of the team. Whenever we can get our players talking to each other, it helps develop bonds between them. It is only when they care about each other that they will make an extra effort for the team.

PLAYBOOK EXERCISE

- Evaluate your team's spirit. What are the positive signs that you see? Who is responsible for them?
- What are the less-than-positive things you see? Who is responsible for them?

NEXT STEP

- Determine a strategy for turning the negatives into positives and a timetable for action. Will you need someone to help you?

5.2 THE CHALLENGES

Coaches face many challenges in trying to meld a number of different individuals and personalities into one team. Unfortunately, there is no one way or easy solution to these challenges. Nothing tests a person's coaching ability more than how the coach overcomes these issues that every coach and team faces.

EGOS AND PERSONALITY TYPES

Kobe Bryant and Shaquille O'Neill were teammates on the Los Angeles Lakers for years. Both players are Hall of Fame athletes and both had huge egos. Sports writers continually debated about whose team the Lakers were—were they Kobe's or Shaq's? Each player considered himself the most important member of the team. Should the offense be built around Kobe or around Shaq?

Phil Jackson was hired as the Lakers coach at least in part because of his ability to get great players to be willing to play for the team and not for themselves. In professional sports the problem of ego gets written about a great deal, and it is a common problem. But it is not restricted to professional sports. From the youngest levels of sports there are those athletes who want to score, who want to play offense but not defense, who think they know better than others the way the team should function.

Everyone's leadership style is different. Some are aggressive, others are passive; some are vocal, others are quiet; some are disciplined, others are not; some are positive, others are negative. Bringing a diverse group of individuals into a cohesive team is a challenge. The successful coach is the person who recognizes and celebrates differences, and who helps each person understand how he or she is a part of the whole.

PERSONALITY CONFLICTS

When Lou Holtz became the head football coach at the University of South Carolina, he quickly turned the program around. How did he do it? The first thing he did was take the entire team on a one-week retreat during which they did not play any football. Instead, in a very structured way, the players got to know each other—where they were from, who their family members were, what their backgrounds were, the music they liked, the TV shows they followed, the way they approached life. His goal was simple. If the players got to know and like each other, they would come together as a team and play for each other.

It is inevitable that there will be individuals who do not like or get along well with others, and this is a challenge that comes with every team. Most coaches are too afraid to sacrifice a week of practice as Holtz did, but not to deal with personality issues is to foreclose on the possibility of the team reaching its full potential.

PLAYBOOK EXERCISE

- Identify a few examples of when you have been an asset to team play and when you have hindered team play.
- What personality conflicts have you had to deal with in the past? How did you handle them? What would you do differently now?

NEXT STEP

- Write out a strategy for dealing with egotistical players and for dealing with a personality conflict.

INJURIES AND BAD LUCK

Few things are more demoralizing to a team than to have one of its best players injured or to lose a game as the result of a freak play. Yet, both of these things are common in sports. A twisted knee. A torn muscle. A broken bone. A Hail Mary pass. A bad bounce. A lucky shot. A once-in-a-lifetime play. All of these combine to challenge a team's willingness to continue to make their best effort.

In his poem *If*, Kipling wrote that you are growing up "If you can meet with triumph and disaster and treat those two imposters just the same..." Disaster often strikes as an odds-defying event. Kipling's advice is to be able to meet both triumph and disaster equally, and above all to recognize that they are both "imposters."

> If you can meet with triumph and disaster and treat those two imposters just the same...
> — Rudyard Kipling

What is an imposter? An imposter is someone who pretends to be someone that he or she is not. Kipling is imploring us to recognize that neither victory nor defeat is as important as it pretends to be. We are not to have our lives shaped by imposters. We are to accept injuries, bad calls, fluke plays, and the whims of sport with equanimity, knowing that whether we win or lose, victory or defeat is not as important as how we got there.

The relationships we make are also not "just a game," for these are the things that really matter, these are the things that endure, and these are the things that make life meaningful and beautiful.

The successful people are those prepared for adversity, even disaster, before it happens so that when it comes—and no matter what form it takes—they are prepared as if they had expected it to happen. They are also able to see beyond the moment to the relationships that are enduring.

> The successful people are those prepared for adversity... so that when it comes...they are prepared as if they had expected it to happen.

COACHING STRATEGY

All good athletes think they know how to win. They think they know what offense or defense should be used, or what combination of players or positions for players would work best. In other words, players often think they know as well as or better than their coach how the team should be run.

The challenge here is for the coach to communicate well with the team. The team needs to know how and why the coach has made the decisions that have been made (why a particular offense or defense has been chosen, for example). The players need to know what the coach's thinking and philosophy is, and how that translates into the team goals.

Equally, the players should have the opportunity to share privately with the coach their own ideas and thoughts, and to have the coach demonstrate the openness and willingness to take those thoughts seriously. By listening to the concerns that individuals may have, the coach shows respect for the player and shows that he or she values the players who are presenting their ideas.

This is particularly true for younger coaches and for coaches with losing teams. Coaches who have a long and successful record will usually have their methods accepted by their players. But those coaches who are new or who have had losing seasons are more apt to have their credentials questioned by those who play and those who observe. Not surprisingly, when players are able to approach a coach with ideas, have those ideas listened to honestly and respectfully, and have the rationale for decisions communicated, the players will almost invariably become more committed to the coach and the team, whether the ideas are accepted or not.

5.3 BENEFITS OF TEAM PLAY

PLAYING AS A TEAM

One of the great experiences of sports is to play as a team. When the team comes together as one, each person realizes and values the contribution of the others and knows that each is an important part of the whole. Moreover, when the team knows it won because of the coordinated effort of everyone rather than because of simply having superior athletes, it is one of the most satisfying moments in competition. Equally, when the team knows it played its best, there is a sense of satisfaction even in defeat. There is no dishonor or regret when one is beaten by a better team.

THE RELATIONSHIPS

When Lou Gehrig was forced to retire because of his terminal illness, his words became one of the most famous speeches in sports history. Dying of the disease that would become known by his name, he said, "Today I consider myself the luckiest man on the face of the earth."

Why did a dying man, struck down at a young age, consider himself "the luckiest man on the face of the earth?" Read what he said on July 4, 1939, at Yankee Stadium on Lou Gehrig Appreciation Day and you will see why:

"Fans, for the past two weeks you have been reading about a bad break I got. Yet today I consider myself the luckiest man on the face of the earth. I have been in ballparks for seventeen years and I have never received anything but kindness and encouragement from you fans. Look at these grand men. Which of you wouldn't consider it the highlight of his career just to associate with them for even one day? Sure, I'm lucky. Who wouldn't have considered it an honor to have known Jacob Ruppert? Also, the builder of baseball's greatest empire, Ed Barrow? To have spent six years with that wonderful little fellow, Miller Huggins? Then to have spent the next nine years with that outstanding leader, that smart student of psychology, the best manager in baseball today, Joe McCarthy? Sure, I'm lucky. When the New York Giants, a team you would give your right arm to beat, and vice versa, sends you a gift, that's something. When everybody down to the groundskeeper and those boys in white coats remember you with trophies, that's something. When you have a father and mother work all their lives so that you can have an education and build your body, it's a blessing. When you have a wife who has been a tower of strength and shown more courage than you dreamed existed, that's the finest I know. I consider myself the luckiest man on the face of the earth. And I might have been given a bad break, but I've got an awful lot to live for."

The relationships he made through sports and with his family meant everything to him.

Many of the bonds of friendship are forged on the athletic field. When we practice together, train together, play together, struggle together, win together and lose together, we learn what it is to be together, to be together as one. The commitment that we make to the others as a member of the team, reciprocated by the others, leads to life-long friendships and commitments. Over forty years after I graduated from high school, I still think back to the teams I played on and the friendships I shared there as one of the highlights of those days. In many small towns, where high school football is the highlight of the year, former players remain foremost fixed in the town's memory as the players they were, no matter what career may come after.

PLAYBOOK EXERCISE

- What are some of the best teams you've been a part of, in terms of teamwork and unity, not wins and losses? What were some of the worst?
- What were the keys to the good teams? The worst?

NEXT STEP

- Determine one way you can improve the relationships on the team.

CHAPTER 6

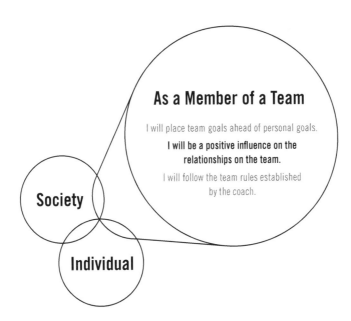

Living The Code as a Member of a Team

As a Member of a Team

I will place team goals ahead of personal goals.

I will be a positive influence on the relationships on the team.

I will follow the team rules established by the coach.

Society

Individual

THE SECOND TENET

Team spirit is dependent on every member of the team working together, seeking to build a spirit of unity and purpose. Relationships between team members and coaches are critical if the team is to become a real "team." In this chapter we will explore the building blocks of relationships and look into the challenges and rewards of meaningful relationships with others. Our chapter is organized as follows:

"I will be a positive influence on the relationships on the team."

6.1 Learning to Love
6.2 Communication and the Art of Listening
    Learn to Listen
    Listen for Feelings
    Active Listening
6.3 Learning to Be a Cheerleader: The Art of Encouraging
    Look for Little Things
    Speak in Front of Others as Well as in Private
    Model the Behavior You Expect from Others
6.4 Learning to Confront Others: The Art of Dealing with Conflict
    Identify the Conflict
    Determine a Time to Deal with It
    Confront the Other Person in a Non-confrontational Way
    Set Ground Rules for Discussion
    Make "I" Statements
6.5 Learning to Reconcile: The Art of Giving and Receiving Forgiveness
    Find Common Ground
    Identify, Respect, and Honor the Feelings of the Other Person
    Make Sure Each Person Can Articulate the Other's Viewpoint
    Look for a Win-Win Solution; Make the Goal Clear
6.6 Learning to Apologize: The Art of Taking Responsibility
    Learn to Accept an Apology
    Learn the Power of Forgiveness
6.7 Five Keys to Building Positive Relationships
    Trust
    Mutual Commitment
    Willingness to Sacrifice

6.1 LEARNING TO LOVE

A counselor friend of mine once offered a course entitled, "Learning to Love." It was completely full almost immediately. It was filled with both married couples and single people. Something about the title struck a nerve. We are all trying to learn how to love. In other words, we are all trying to learn how to build meaningful relationships that will endure. How do we say "You are important" or "I disagree with you" or "You made a mistake" or "I am sorry" so that it builds the relationship in a positive direction? As we get older we learn how important this is in all the relationships in our lives—our families, our jobs, and our teams. To completely compose our characters, we all need to learn to love.

> How do we say, "You are important" or "I disagree with you" or "You made a mistake" or "I am sorry" so that it builds the relationship in a positive direction?

In this chapter we will explore the main principles we need to remember as we all strive to be positive influences in our relationships with others.

PLAYBOOK EXERCISE

- Would you have signed up for the course?
- How would you assess your own ability to communicate with others?
- How would others assess your ability?

NEXT STEP

- Write down one or two ways you would like to improve your ability to communicate that you care to others, and a timeline for getting there.

6.2 COMMUNICATION AND THE ART OF LISTENING

All relationships begin, continue, and end with communication. Unfortunately, it is often not good communication, and poor communication can be hurtful and destructive. Even those who care about each other may end up arguing about things in ways that undermine their relationship. Good communication requires work and discipline, just like any other skill. Here are the components we need to practice:

LEARN TO LISTEN

As children we all were told, "You have two ears and one mouth; that's because it's more important to listen than to speak." There is some truth in that. But it's also true that just listening is not enough. To listen to the other person, we have to care about and value the other person. We can be "listening" without really hearing! We can tell if people are truly interested in what we have to say or if they are just letting us talk. It takes effort to listen to many people. We need to acknowledge that and determine that we will make the effort.

The difficult task of "just listening" reminds us that:

- We are not listening if we are thinking about our response while someone is still talking.
- We are not listening if we are thinking that we have already heard this before and know what we think about it.
- We are listening if we are giving the speaker our full attention.
- We are listening if we ask follow-up questions to test our understanding or to elicit more information.

LISTEN FOR FEELINGS

We all have thoughts and feelings. Our thoughts and opinions are important to us. Usually that is the level at which we speak: "I think we need to work harder." Or, "I don't think everyone gave the best effort."

Thoughts are important, but feelings have more power. Great speakers generate and connect with the feelings within us. Whenever we can tap into the feelings of others, we are tapping into their hearts.

An important first step is attempting to identify the feelings of the speaker. A teammate might say, "We all have to do our best, and I don't think we did our best yesterday," but what is he or she really saying? Is it, "I'm disappointed," or "I'm mad," or "I'm really talking to just one person," or "I'm better than you," or what? In response, you could say, "I agree with you. We need to do our best." But, it would probably be better if you said, "It sounds to me like you're angry," or "disappointed," or "frustrated." That is, it would be better if you could try to identify the feeling. This would allow the speaker to say, "Yes, I am angry because..." The answer may not be as you assumed (as we will see later). It's usually more helpful to talk about feelings than thoughts.

Many men have more difficulty talking about their feelings than women do. Generally, men have traditionally been culturally raised to be tough, in-control, goal-oriented, and not given to caring about their feelings. Their feelings are to be suppressed, and the focus is always on the object or the goal, not on any "sissy" feelings they may have. It is hard for many men to express their feelings because they are not in touch with them. They may be mad but not understand why. For example, a player might blow up at a teammate because he's mad the team lost. But that mad feeling may not just be because the game was lost; it may have come from weeks earlier when that teammate missed practice or didn't take a particular technique seriously. Now, when the game is lost, all that past feeling erupts. How much better it would have been had the player identified his feelings and said, "I'm really mad because I'm frustrated, because you have goofed off in practice for weeks." How much better things could have turned out if that player had been able to express his feelings by saying something similar weeks earlier when he became upset!

Or, a player might be upset after a loss because he or she always wanted to have an undefeated season and now that goal will not be achieved. So, in this case, the player is not so much angry as sad and disappointed that he or she will not be able to hit an important goal.

I asked a player who played for Bear Bryant, when the Bear was an assistant coach at Kentucky, what it was like to play for him. His answer was, "He would come over to your room at night to be sure you were doing okay on your homework, and if you needed help, he'd stay with you." What is he really saying? What are the feelings behind the words? It is told in the form of information, of what the Bear did. But what is really being said is that the Bear *cared* and the player had feelings of love as a result. I said to this player, "It sounds like you really liked the Bear because you felt that he really cared about you." His response: "You bet he did, and that's why we all played for him!" The player's willingness to give his best for the coach was related to his feelings that the coach cared about him.

So, listening for feelings involves listening for the feeling that is behind the words being spoken. It also involves listening for the feelings that are stirred up inside us, identifying them, and then trying to figure out why we have those feelings. For example, just mentioning the names Arnold Palmer, Dennis Rodman, Pete Rose, or Peyton Manning conjures up different reactions within us. What are the feelings that go with those reactions? Where do those feelings come from? Our own feelings often come from places we do not realize at first. When we learn how to identify what our own feelings are, we begin to learn who we are. As we learn who we are, we can work to see things differently, then we can change and grow as we are able to see areas needing improvement.

ACTIVE LISTENING

A key technique to learn is what is called "active listening." It is called "active" because rather than just allowing a person to talk, we actively check out what we think we are hearing, by testing for feeling. Here's an example:

Person one: Coach was really on us today. Made us do extra wind sprints.

Person two: Sounds like you're a little mad with the coach.

Person one: Yes, I am; we should be doing extra drills, not sprints.

In this case, we tested our assumption about the feeling ("Sounds like you're mad") and were confirmed in it.

Here's another way it could have gone:
Person one: Coach was really on us today. Made us do extra wind sprints.
Person two: Sounds like you're a little mad with the coach.
Person one: No, I'm not. I'm glad he did. We need better conditioning.

In this case, we tested our assumption about the feeling ("Sounds like you're mad") and found out we were wrong. If we do not engage in active listening, in testing our assumptions, we may misunderstand what is being said. This happens all the time, as the last example shows.

Another example:
Person one: Coach Jones doesn't know what he's doing.
Person two: Sure he does; he's won two state titles.
Person one: No, he's a moron.

Here's another way it could have gone:
Person one: Coach Jones doesn't know what he's doing.
Person two: Sounds like you're really mad at him.
Person one: I sure am. He won't let me try another position.

By listening for feelings, we learn why our teammate is mad at the coach. If we had pursued our first instinct, to defend the coach, we might not have learned why our friend was mad at the coach.

By participating actively, we are checking out the feelings of the speaker. When we respond, we need to try to respond to the feelings, not to the words themselves. We can always come back to the words, but the feelings are the key point.

PLAYBOOK EXERCISE

- Would others say that you are a good listener?
- Are you able to identify the feelings you have at any given time?

- Did you understand "active listening?" Have you ever practiced it?

NEXT STEPS

- Determine a relationship you are going to work on.
- Practice "active listening" intentionally for one day. What surprised you the most in doing it?

6.3 LEARNING TO BE A CHEERLEADER: THE ART OF ENCOURAGING

We all benefit by being encouraged in whatever we are undertaking. Tennis great Althea Gibson said that no one ever became a champion without having a key person who believed in and encouraged him or her. We all need people who believe in us and stand with us no matter how we perform on any one day. Positive energy generates positive responses from others.

To help create positive relationships on the team, each person must do his or her part to contribute to the whole. Encouraging and cheerleading must be genuine. Empty words are understood as such and create a negative experience for others. Here are some key tips to practice as we seek to be encouragers on our team:

LOOK FOR LITTLE THINGS

Maintaining positive relationships requires ongoing effort. It's important to look for the little ways we can encourage and support others. The obvious thing is to commend things that are typically taken for granted, such as a good pass or a special effort. A key in this is to actively look for ways to be positive. We can also be positive by asking about *things we can't see*. For example, a simple "How are things going for you?" asked in a way that communicates real interest may lead to an important conversation about a personal issue unrelated to sports. All the bonds of friendship that are built will ultimately strengthen the team.

SPEAK IN FRONT OF OTHERS AS WELL AS IN PRIVATE

Learning to share a kind word and to look for opportunities to encourage others is an important way to maintain and develop our friendships and relationships. While this will often happen one-on one or in the presence of one or two others, it is important to look for ways to commend others publicly, such as in front of the whole team. There are always key moments when a particular word spoken or person acknowledged can make a significant difference. Most importantly, we should always be sincere in what we say. Idle "rah-rah" chatter will be understood as insincere and should be avoided. In that way, when something is important and we want to be heard, our words will carry real weight. Remember the story of the boy who cried wolf? No one wants to be that boy!

MODEL THE BEHAVIOR YOU EXPECT FROM OTHERS

There is an old saying, "I'd rather see a sermon than hear one." The truth is that what we do is more important than our words; our daily actions establish our credibility. The person who slacks off in practice and gives less than 100 percent in a game will have no credibility if he or she says, "Let's go, we can do it!" On the other hand, the person who has already earned the respect and admiration of teammates will be heard. Be the sermon.

PLAYBOOK EXERCISE

- Would your friends describe you as an encourager?
- What are the ways you think you encourage others?

- What are the ways you fail to encourage others?

NEXT STEPS

- Determine a strategy for becoming more of an encourager.
- Include one way that you can model the behavior you expect from others.
- Set a date to evaluate your efforts.

6.4 LEARNING TO CONFRONT OTHERS: THE ART OF DEALING WITH CONFLICT

Conflict is inevitable when you have a group of individuals who are motivated and committed to achieving a goal as a team. This is natural because personalities are all different and because we approach things in different ways. Conflict is not necessarily a bad thing. Handled properly, it can create conversation that leads to clarity and focus for those involved—and to greater commitment as well.

It is always better to be proactive in any situation involving conflict. Things rarely, if ever, "simply go away." Feelings and emotions that are suppressed will always have a way of coming out, usually in unfortunate ways and at inopportune times.

Here are some steps to take in any situation:

IDENTIFY THE CONFLICT

Determine if there is an issue between one or more team members. Sometimes it's obvious; other times it may be something that is under the surface, unspoken, but destructive. If one person harbors feelings for another, it will reveal itself in indirect (if not direct) ways. Those negative feelings will always surface, either passive-aggressively or in the form of a team that lacks positive energy and chemistry.

DETERMINE A TIME TO DEAL WITH IT

There is a time and a place for everything. Public blowups usually result in bigger hurts and bigger problems that often could have been avoided with some forethought. In any event, conflicts are best resolved in an appropriate atmosphere.

CONFRONT THE OTHER PERSON IN A NON-CONFRONTATIONAL WAY

It is important to approach people that are having a conflict in a way that does not make them defensive or angry. In many ways, the approach may have a lot to do with how successful you are going to be. If it is handled poorly, it will only make things worse. Here are some suggested ways of approaching someone, all of which are intended to open up lines of communication:

"I have something important I want to talk about."

"I need to talk to you sometime when it's good for you."

"Could we get together some time? There's something bothering me and I'd like to talk about it."

When the other person says, "What is it?" resist the temptation to tell them! Just say, "I'd like to wait until we have time to talk about it." In other words, unless you have time to sit down for at least 30 minutes with the door shut, do not try to do it quickly just to get it over with.

SET GROUND RULES FOR THE DISCUSSION

When you do meet, start by setting the ground rules for discussion. This is particularly necessary if you have two or more people present who are having a conflict with each other.

MAKE "I" STATEMENTS

This is very important. When we make "I" statements we begin the sentence with "I," and so we only focus on ourselves and how we feel. We do not try to describe what other people are doing or saying; we only say how it affects us. Rather than saying "You always say X," it is better to say, "I get angry when I see or hear X." By only making "I" statements we are able to let everyone know how their information and viewpoints have been heard. We do not talk about what we think is going on in another person's head. We only talk about how we feel, or felt, when something happens or has happened.

No language that attacks or demeans another is permitted.

Each person gets to speak without being interrupted.

We will continue this process in the next section.

PLAYBOOK EXERCISE

- This chapter has outlined a process for beginning to deal with conflict. Do you agree with it? In what ways do you disagree?
- Analyze how you have handled conflicts in the past.
- What will your strategy be to deal with a conflict you are facing now?

NEXT STEPS

- Ask a few friends how they think you do in handling conflict. Practice your listening skills as they speak.
- What is something important that you have learned or been reminded of?

6.5 LEARNING TO RECONCILE: THE ART OF GIVING AND RECEIVING FORGIVENESS

FIND COMMON GROUND

The starting point to conflict resolution should be finding the common ground on which we stand. By this we mean that we are all on the same team, we all want to be successful, and we are all committed to that effort. It is important for each person to recognize and affirm those common desires. This section includes some ways you can help others when a conflict arises.

IDENTIFY, RESPECT, AND HONOR THE FEELINGS OF THE OTHER PERSON(S)

It is not always easy to identify the feelings or the problem. Several issues may have become layered on top of one another. The real source of the feelings of anger or hostility may or may not be easy to determine. However, it is important to work as hard as possible to articulate the feelings and actions that have brought on this conflict. All thoughts and feelings should be symbolically laid out on a table in a non-judgmental way.

MAKE SURE EACH PERSON CAN ARTICULATE THE OTHER'S VIEWPOINT

After each person has shared his or her thoughts and feelings, ask each person to repeat what the other person said. It is important that it is repeated as it was originally shared, without any comments. For example, if the second person does not articulate what the first said, then the first should repeat it until the first is satisfied that the second has understood it correctly.

LOOK FOR A WIN-WIN SOLUTION; MAKE THE GOAL CLEAR

Ask if each understands why the other is conflicted. When they have agreed that each understands the other, then the question becomes, what do we have to do to work this out? Let them know that you are looking for a win-win solution. It may be that one person needs to apologize; it may be that both need to apologize. However, apologizing does not necessarily guarantee success. The apology must be accepted by the other, and sometimes this is not easily granted. In some cases, more than an apology may be warranted.

6.6 LEARNING TO APOLOGIZE: THE ART OF TAKING RESPONSIBILITY

It is usually difficult to apologize. It means admitting that we made a mistake. But healing cannot take place in a relationship or on a team as long as something is broken. It needs to be fixed. Often, situations have gotten complicated, with more than one person responsible for the situation, and so one person does not want to apologize if that person thinks that others are being let off the hook. However, one person does not have to take the responsibility for the whole conflict, but can take responsibility for his or her part. It should be easy to say, "I am sorry for my part in all of this. What I did was wrong and so I am sorry that I did what I did, or said what I said." Even if we did not cause the conflict, if we played any part, however small, we should regret it and be willing to offer our apology.

One person does not have to take the responsibility for the whole conflict, but can take responsibility for his or her part.

LEARNING TO ACCEPT AN APOLOGY IS A NECESSARY STEP

When others are willing to humble themselves and admit that they made a mistake for which they are sorry, we should always be willing to forgive them. At times this is difficult to do because we may have been hurt very badly, and even an apology cannot heal a deep wound easily. However, it is good to remember that we are all imperfect, and that by apologizing, the other person is acknowledging that he or she has flaws and is asking to be forgiven. Recognizing the truth of that may help make it easier for us to accept the apology and to know that we all share a common humanity.

LEARNING THE POWER OF FORGIVENESS TO HEAL RELATIONSHIPS

In a famous speech in *The Merchant of Venice*, Shakespeare's Portia says that mercy is "twice blessed," because it blesses the person who gives it and the person who receives it. This is so true of forgiveness. When we have been in conflict with another, when we are able to forgive and be forgiven, we discover a new life, a new energy. The act of forgiving touches both people, and indeed its power will carry over to the whole team.

PLAYBOOK EXERCISE

- Write down your thoughts on forgiveness. When was a time you were forgiven?
- Can you think of a significant time when you forgave someone?
- What were your feelings before, during, and after the discussion of forgiveness?

NEXT STEPS

- Determine a person you need to forgive and how you will do it.
- Put down a date by which you will have taken that next step.

6.7 FIVE KEYS TO BUILDING POSITIVE RELATIONSHIPS

Communication is the key to all relationships, and the challenge of learning to communicate in a clear and effective way cannot be overstated. There are five additional keys to test ourselves against and to work to improve on all the time. We have touched on some of these points in previous chapters, but it is good to remember them in this context.

TRUST

We, teammates and coaches, must be able to trust each other. Trust means that we will be honest with each other, that we will do the things we commit to doing, and that we will never betray or undermine the other in any way. This is tough because players and coaches like to talk to each other about others; it is easy to want to make ourselves look better by saying something negative about someone else.

MUTUAL COMMITMENT

Commit to each other and to the goals of the team. To have positive relationships on the team, everyone must be committed to the team goals. If it is clear that someone is not committed in this way, or has other conflicts, this must be dealt with by everyone.

WILLINGNESS TO SACRIFICE

On the other side of the commitment coin, our commitment to each other and to the well-being of the team is measured by our willingness to do all we can to help our team succeed.

CONTINUAL WORK

Developing relationships takes continual work. Like any skill, relationship building must be practiced daily, refined and developed. New skills and techniques can always be learned. There are many days when we don't feel like practicing, but as in any skill development, those are the days we have to will ourselves to continue.

HONEST COMMUNICATION

Communication is the key, as we have said. But it can be misused as well. To be a positive influence, we must always resist the temptation to manipulate others. Few things are more tempting than trying to manipulate someone into doing something or believing something. People who manipulate one person usually will do it to others as well, and those affected will eventually realize that they were not being dealt with honestly. Then trust and the relationship are damaged, if not destroyed.

PLAYBOOK EXERCISE

- Are you a person others can trust? What evidence do you have for or against your response?
- Do you think everyone is willing to make the same commitment to the team? Can you measure it?
- Do you think you are honest and straightforward in your dealings with others? What would they say? Why?

NEXT STEPS

- Determine a relationship you would like to work on.
- Develop a plan for several different ways you can work on this relationship in the coming weeks. Try to put down clear and measurable objectives so that you can judge how you have done.

6.8 PRACTICAL ISSUES

A number of practical issues relate to maintaining positive relationships on the team. It is important to consider them separately.

OUR OWN NEEDS AND WANTS

No matter who we are, we need to know what it is that we want and expect out of others; we also must know what we will get from them. If we have expectations that others are not aware of, our relationships will soon sour. We have talked about this under the rules established by the coach, but it is important in every aspect of being on a team.

THE ROLE OF THE CAPTAIN

The captain has the opportunity to serve as a leader of the team. It is possible that every player can play a leadership role at various times, and many do, but it is the expectation that the captain will serve as both official and unofficial leader of the team. The captain should play a role that is natural and consistent with his or her personality rather than try to emulate some imagined role. If the captain's behavior is consistent with who he or she is, the captain should play a significant role in developing the unity, cohesiveness, and spirit of the team.

BULLYING

It should be unnecessary to bring this up. However, bullying has become such a large problem in today's schools that we wish to address it. Coaches should make it clear to their teams that no form of bullying, teasing, or abuse of any member of the team by anyone at any time in any place will be tolerated. Further, given the situation in so many schools, the expectation should be that all players will be proactive in sticking up and standing with any teammate (or anyone!) who is ever the subject of any form of bullying by anyone, no matter where it occurs.

PLAYBOOK EXERCISE

- How would you describe the relationships on your team?
- Can you identify any individual or group on your team that causes your team to be divided in any way?

NEXT STEPS

- Identify the member of your team that you dislike the most or who gives you the most trouble.
- Work out a plan for improving your relationship with this member of the team.

CHAPTER 7

Living The Code as a Member of a Team

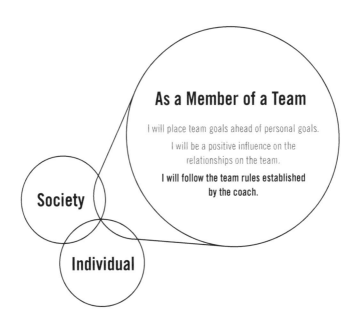

As a Member of a Team

I will place team goals ahead of personal goals.

I will be a positive influence on the relationships on the team.

I will follow the team rules established by the coach.

Society

Individual

THE THIRD TENET

Order, discipline, and a coordinated effort by the entire team is the responsibility of the coach. One of the keys to the coach's leadership is the rules established by the coach. They often set the tone and the character of the team. We will explore this tenet in the following way:

"I will follow the team rules established by the coach."

7.1 FREEDOM AND AUTHORITY

When we are children we all want to be free from the control of our parents. We cannot do all the things we want to be able to do, and we long for freedom. Freedom comes in the form of a driver's license for many teenagers. It's the first time they are not dependent on their parents to take them wherever they want to go. When we first do something by ourselves, we are thrilled with the new feeling of freedom that we experience.

We soon learn that there is no such thing as freedom, that while being free means we are free to choose, we must live with our choices. Freedom is a burden. We have to choose how we spend every second of our lives. It is no longer our parents telling us what we cannot do; we are choosing what we will do.

Freedom is a burden.

So, how do we make our choices? At first, we do the things we want to do, that others do, or that we were taught. It begins as an unthinking process. For some people this process can go on for a very long time. Sooner or later, however, we realize that we have to decide who we will become as a person. What are our values? What will our character look like?

The question that stands behind and within these questions is, what authority do we recognize? Authority is an important word. By it we mean, what is it that governs our lives? Are we always going to do only what is best for us? Or, are we only going to do what is best for others? When we decide, what is the basis for our decision?

What authority do we recognize?

In other words, we are asking, "What is your Code for Living?"

As we have already observed, there are many different codes for living. Religious beliefs, cultural traditions, family values, and civic duties all make up overlapping value systems through which we forge our identity by making our choices.

We all need to live under authority. This is not what we want to hear or believe. We want to be our own authority. But those who try to live alone and without authority set themselves up for their own downfall, whether as an individual, in a family, in a business, or in a career. Those who break the legal authority will be brought to justice, and those who have no moral authority often will see their lives self-destruct sooner or later.

ABW does not seek to discourage any of the personal beliefs or faith traditions of anyone. In fact, we encourage everyone to consider seriously all the sources of meaning and value that are, can, or should be a part of their lives. The purpose of The Code is to provide common ground on which we can all stand, no matter what our personal faith or value system may be. The Code, as an authority in our lives, reflects beliefs and values that we have already accepted from our own faith tradition, our parents, or other people we respect and admire. In any event, we need to build our lives under an authority (or authorities) greater than ourselves.

PLAYBOOK EXERCISE

- Make a list of the authorities you recognize in your life.
- Put down the evidence others would see for the authorities in your life.

NEXT STEPS

- Choose an authority that you would like to make a bigger part of your life.
- Determine a measurable strategy for making this happen.

7.2 LAWS AND RULES

In the United States we consider ourselves to be a free people. We have the freedom to choose our religion, to say whatever we wish, to travel and move wherever we desire, and to make our own decisions. Our freedom, however, is not limitless. The courts have determined that we can exercise our freedom as Americans only insofar as it does not interfere with another person's freedom. For example, we have speed limits on the highway to help ensure that people arrive safely at their destinations. And while we have freedom of speech, we cannot yell "fire, fire!" in a crowded theatre because that may result in a stampede that could harm others. We can travel on an airplane, but we will have to be searched first so any potentially harmful items can be discovered and confiscated.

We can exercise our freedom as Americans only insofar as it does not interfere with another person's freedom.

The authority of the law provides for order and safety in society. In the military, the chain of command provides an authority for order. The boss provides for order in the workplace. The parent provides for order in the home.

7.3 ONLY ONE CAPTAIN ON THE SHIP

When I was eleven years old I learned to sail. Sailing is a wonderful sport but totally dependent on teamwork. When three eleven-year-olds are in a sailboat race, only one is the skipper (the captain). It is not unusual for one to think that he or she has a better strategy for winning the race. This results in an argument! There can only be one skipper, and the skipper's orders have to be followed or the boat cannot compete. If a captain gives an order to a crew member, the execution of that is usually time sensitive. Any delay or hesitation is time lost. Once this lesson is learned, the crew member learns never to ask "why?" at the time an order is given, but only later, when there is time for a constructive conversation.

The coach is the authority on the team, the person who provides order. When the authority of the coach is accepted and honored, the team has its best chance for success. This does not mean that the strategies, methods, or systems that the coach employs cannot be discussed. The coach's authority is enhanced by openness to the ideas of suggestions of others. But there is a time and a place for everything.

All good coaches have rules for their team. Depending on the sport and the team, there are usually a variety of rules: training rules, practice rules, off-the-field rules, and travel rules. Some coaches will include academic rules. Some rules are obvious, such as being on time to practice. Others are less obvious. For example, when traveling, the coach might require a dress code that is more formal than normal school dress. Perhaps this is so the team can look good when they travel together, or it could be because the coach is seeking to add another layer of pride, identity, and bonding to the team.

THE COACH AS THE AUTHORITY

In joining a team, we agree to submit to the authority of the coach. At times this is easy, and at other times it can be challenging. What do we do when we disagree with the coach? The good coach, like any good leader, will make it known how and how not to raise questions. As a member of the team, each person must follow the rules established by the coach.

PLAYBOOK EXERCISE

- Write down a few examples of when you followed the directions of others with which you disagreed.
- In what ways are you a good follower? In what ways are you not a good follower?
- Do you think a chain of command is a good thing in every situation? If not, in what situations is an alternative method better?

NEXT STEP

- Determine at least one way that you can demonstrate to others your commitment to the direction of your coach.

7.4 EXPLAINING THE RULES

When John Wooden was the basketball coach at UCLA he began every year with a lesson in how to put on socks and shoes. You can imagine how the players reacted! Some were All-Americans and all of them had been putting on socks and shoes most of their lives. But Wooden was insistent on this ritual every year because he did not want any of his players to develop blisters if the socks were improperly put on. In doing this, I am sure that the players also learned the importance of details—and the kind of attention to detail that their coach expected of them. Explaining his way of putting on the socks and shoes also taught them how they were to approach every aspect of being on that team.

Nothing breeds grumbling easier than asking young people to do something they don't see any reason to do. When we have asked an authority figure why we should do something, we have all heard at one time or another, "Because I said so!" And that has at times confused or angered us. At a minimum, we need to understand why we are being asked to do things. We may disagree with the value, but at least we will understand the thinking behind the request.

Players will all understand the importance of being at practice on time and of supporting each other, but some may not understand the training rules or practices of the coach. It is important for the coach to take the time at the beginning of the year to articulate his or her philosophy as expressed through the rules (and other expectations for the team).

7.5 PERSONAL HONESTY: HONORING THE RULES

Many of the coach's rules can be easily followed, but some can be easily broken. There is an old saying, "Discipline is what you do when no one is watching." No one knows if you break a training rule by having an alcoholic drink in your room or staying up too late. But you know. What you have is more than a rules violation; it is a failure to do your duty, to live up to what is possible and best in you. It is your failure to live up to your commitment to the team.

Discipline is what you do when no one is watching.

Failure in the small things is as important as failure in the big things. We do not naturally see things that way all the time. We want to believe that our character is determined based on the truly important things. But it is more likely that the opposite is true. The person who honors the smallest commitment, who attends to the smallest detail, who seeks to do his or her best in the small things will more likely be consistent with the large things. The one who slacks off in small things is not as disciplined and as conditioned to carry through on the big things. If we can win the small battles and succeed in the daily challenges, then we will forge a character that is solid from the bottom up.

PLAYBOOK EXERCISE

- Do you and your team understand the reason for your rules?
- Are there any rules that cause difficulty for others?
- How do the spirit and the letter of the rules differ?

NEXT STEP

- Determine at least two ways you can better honor the rules in your situation.

7.6 LIVING INTO FREEDOM AND OBEDIENCE

The irony of having an authority over us is that it frees us as it limits us. When we choose the direction for our life, the authority we must recognize will become clear. When we submit to that authority, it will provide the blueprint on which we can then build a successful life. The Code for Living reminds us that we are going to do our best, we are going to respect others, we are going to play by the rules, and we are going to put team goals ahead of our personal goals. These are all the markers on the path to a fulfilled life, a life with meaning and purpose.

CHAPTER 8

Living The Code as a Member of Society

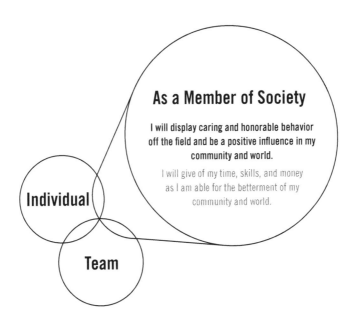

As a Member of Society

I will display caring and honorable behavior off the field and be a positive influence in my community and world.

I will give of my time, skills, and money as I am able for the betterment of my community and world.

Individual

Team

THE FIRST TENET

We come now to the final section of The Code, which outlines our responsibility as citizens of our country and members of society. Some of the values that have already been articulated will reappear in this section, but this is to be expected for a simple reason: We should live lives of consistency. In other words, the values that determine how we will act as individuals, or as members of a team, will inevitably also come into play as we reflect on our role off the field and in the community. This chapter is organized this way:

"I will display caring and honorable behavior off the field and be a positive influence in my community and world."

8.1 When You Know Who You Are, You Know How to Act
8.2 Excellence Should Always Be the Standard
8.3 Displaying Caring and Honorable Behavior
8.4 Being a Positive Influence

8.1 WHEN YOU KNOW WHO YOU ARE, YOU KNOW HOW TO ACT

My father said these words to me on more than one occasion. The primary purpose of this book has been to help us compose our character, to forge who we are, to determine the values that are important to us and to live them out by making them visible to others. It's true: When we know who we are, we will know how to act. It's also true that "growing up" or "forming our character" is something that begins when we are young but is never fully completed. Hopefully, we will continue to grow and mature throughout our lives. Until the day she died, I think my mother kept watching me for signs of improvement!

When we go through our adolescent years we are particularly focused on discovering our individuality. Who are we? How are we going to act? We try out different clothes, haircuts, types of music and so on. Do we wear the same kind of clothes that everyone else does, or the ones we like? Do we try to act like others? Or do we try to think things through, and try to choose our own way? Everyone wants to be unique, but everyone also wants to have friends. If we are "different," we are afraid we may not fit in, and so there is great pressure to conform.

These are questions that every young person faces. But it's also true that many adults never get completely past these adolescent fears of being left out, of having no friends, and of being in some ways "out of it." This is why they follow the fashion pages, read the gossip columns, listen to radio and television talk shows, and do all they can to keep up with whatever the Joneses are doing.

PLAYBOOK EXERCISE

- When have you have tried to conform to what your friends were doing?
- When do you go against the crowd?
- What is the greatest peer pressure you face?
- Do you think your behavior reflects your values? What would others say?

NEXT STEPS

- What part of your identity would you like to work on next?
- Make a list of ways you can grow in that area.

8.2 EXCELLENCE SHOULD ALWAYS BE THE STANDARD

For several generations, Joe DiMaggio was the epitome of grace and style. He patrolled his retirement years as effortlessly as he had patrolled center field for the Yankees. DiMaggio was a symbol of excellence. It may have come naturally to him, but I am sure he would have said it was never easy. All athletes train for hours each day to become skilled at their sport, and excelling off the field of play also requires training. For the high-profile athlete, learning how to respond to a reporter, a young admirer, or a crowd at a charity event is a skill that can be developed, and it takes the same effort and patience as developing any other skill. The same is true for all of us. We all have to take our presence and influence in the world as seriously as we take our family life or professional life.

> Learning how to respond to a reporter, a young admirer, or a crowd at a charity event is a skill that can be developed, and it takes the same effort and patience as developing any other skill.

There is an old saying "It's better to tell the truth, because then you don't have to remember what story you said to anyone." The same is true for our behavior. If we act in a way that is consistent with who we are, then all we have to do is act naturally. On the other hand, if we like to have loose lips in some situations but not in others, then we have to always be thinking about how we are going to behave: Will it be the loose-lips person or the well-mannered person? Obviously, if we play different roles according to where we are, we're not true to ourselves.

When I was driving the car in high school, another driver did something that angered me. I said in a loud voice, "You idiot!" My father was riding in the front seat. He said, "Don't talk like that. Can you imagine someone you like and admire behaving like that?" My father raised the standard on what he expected out of me, even when I was alone and driving a car.

Coach John Wooden said, "It's more important to have character than to be a character." There is always a temptation to be cute, outrageous, or controversial. Again, it is tempting to act in ways that may not reflect the person we want to be. We have all said the wrong thing at one time or another, something that did not reflect the way we wanted people to think of us!

It's more important to have character than to be a character.
— John Wooden

In Kipling's poem *If*, to which we have referred previously, he lauds the ability to "walk with kings and not lose the common touch." It is a marvelous goal: to be ourselves and comfortable no matter who is around. We need this gift if we are to be a positive influence on others, but the only way we can have it is to know who we are. Self-confidence will allow us to be comfortable anywhere.

If you can walk with kings and not lose the common touch.
— Rudyard Kipling

My grandfather was a wonderful and much-loved Irishman. He loved to laugh, tell jokes, and have fun. But he was of that older generation that, when asked to pose for a picture, would never smile. Instead, he would give you a stoic expression that looked like either a frown or an expression of anger. This was frustrating because we wanted to have a picture of him with his giant smile.

One day we decided to trick him. We had bought a movie camera, and we planned that I would be out on the street, and my wife would go for a walk with him. He was always smiling, so we knew that I could film him talking and smiling as they came up the sidewalk.

Here's what happened: They came down the front walk to the sidewalk, turned, and began walking toward me. But just as they turned, a neighbor with a three-year-old child met them by chance on the sidewalk. The film shows my grandfather speaking to the neighbor and then going down to one knee to shake hands and speak to the little girl. This eighty-five-year-old man stayed there, on one knee, until their conversation was over.

That is "walking with kings and not losing the common touch." But that's who he was—a person who valued everyone and treated all people the same.

I have had the privilege of being with Vince Dooley, the Hall of Fame former football coach and athletic director at the University of Georgia, on a number of occasions. Often we are trying to get somewhere for an appointment. He is immediately recognized in the state of Georgia, no matter where he goes. When he is approached, he always stops and treats everyone as if he or she is important to him. The truth is, Coach Dooley is acting in a way that is consistent with who he is.

I have been with many people of different backgrounds and "importance," and it is always interesting and revealing how different people view themselves and how they treat others.

Stephen Vehslage was a national squash champion. One morning he was talking to a group of young athletes. He asked them all, "What is the most valuable thing you have?" Some answered, "my health," or "my parents," or "a friend" and so on. Vehslage said, "I think the most important thing you have is your name. Your name," he repeated. Then he asked, "Do you ever talk about other people when they're not there?" "Oh yes!" they all responded, "We do it all the time!" Then he asked, "Do you ever wonder what they say about you when you're not there?"

Our reputation is a reflection of our character. Living up to our best selves is the standard of excellence to which we should all naturally aspire. There can be no goal higher than to be held in the high respect and admiration of others. A person's reputation is his or her most valuable asset, and what can take years to establish can be lost in one foolish decision.

I think the most important thing you have is your name.
— Stephen Vehslage, national squash champion

As we have observed throughout this book, our attitude more than anything determines how far we go toward achieving our goals. Henry Ford said, "Whether you think you can or you can't, you're right." We all have different skills and abilities, but it is our attitude that determines our work ethic, and our resolve pushes us to do whatever is necessary to achieve our goals.

I have a friend named John DeFoore, a counselor. He tells the true story of a law firm he went to do some work with. It was one of the largest firms in the country and had been started by one man a number of years before. The man was revered by everyone in the firm because he had started the company by himself and had slowly built it up. DeFoore asked for more information about him. Was he married, was he a civic leader, what was his life like outside of work? The painful answer was that he had been married but had gotten divorced; and, no, he had not played a role outside the firm that anyone could think of. He had worked seven days a week to make this firm the great firm it was. As a matter of fact, he had died at his desk on a Sunday afternoon at age 90. He was discovered by the cleaning woman the next morning.

DeFoore says, "We are all equal in one way: We all have 24 hours in the day. However you spend your time, that's what you'll end up with. If you want to build a great law firm, if you spend your life doing that, that's what you'll end up with. If you want to have friends, if you spend all your time making and being friends, you'll end up with a lot of friends. If you want to make money, if you spend all your time trying to make money, that's what you'll end up with. If you want to be a great coach, if you spend all your time working on being a great coach, that's what you'll end up with. However you spend your time, that's what you'll end up with."

> **However you spend your time, that's what you'll end up with.**
> — John DeFoore

We cannot excel at everything. But we can decide how we are going to spend our time. And then we will know what we are going to end up with.

PLAYBOOK EXERCISE

- Do you think you treat all people the same? Would others agree with your answer?

- Can you name one or more people who treat everyone the same? How can you tell?
- What do you think other people say when your name is spoken?
- Who is a person whose behavior you most admire? What is one of his or her character traits you would like to have?

NEXT STEP

- Make a calendar of how you spend your time for one week, and if it didn't end up the way you wanted, make changes for the next week.

8.3 DISPLAYING CARING AND HONORABLE BEHAVIOR

When we think about our role in our community and world, how would we describe it? Are we active, involved, and committed, or are we passive, uninspired, and disinterested? The Code uses the word "display" to describe the expectation to which we are committing. "Display" means to show, exhibit, or reveal. While this can include private or anonymous acts, it has as its primary meaning something that is done publicly, of which one or more people are aware. So, we are not to be silent, unaffected observers of what is going on, but rather people who visibly demonstrate caring and honorable behavior.

Honorable behavior does not mean that we are to automatically assume a certain position on any subject—or that there is always a right and a wrong view on any subject. It does mean, however, that whatever we say or do will merit the respect of others for the way we speak and conduct ourselves.

Equally, however, we should not assume that to display a certain behavior necessarily assumes that we are vocal leaders. Rather it means that in our public life, we will always conduct ourselves in a way that is viewed as positive, respectful, and understood by all. There may be times when displaying caring and honorable behavior will, nevertheless, serve to make others angry. The most important lesson to be learned is how to disagree without becoming personal. We must always resist the temptation to enter into the culture of gossip, innuendo, and personal attacks on individuals that has become popular on television, on radio talk shows, in politics, and in virtually every aspect of society.

The easiest way to go through life is to go with the flow. This means agreeing with the opinions of others without reflection, and conforming with whatever the majority thinks or believes about anything. There are certainly many times when we may not be interested in issues or problems, but the temptation to "get along by going along" does not challenge us as individuals to become our best selves.

The temptation to "get along by going along" does not challenge us as individuals to become our best selves.

To display caring and honorable behavior can be one thing when we are speaking to sympathetic ears, but it can be a difficult thing when we are in the minority of what we are supporting. Those are the occasions when it requires courage to be true to ourselves.

PLAYBOOK EXERCISE

- When is a time that you tend to go with the flow, when you wish you were more assertive?
- What is one area in which you have displayed honorable and caring behavior?

NEXT STEP

- Each day for the next week, look for an occasion when you can deliberately demonstrate caring and honorable behavior.

8.4 BEING A POSITIVE INFLUENCE

In all of our lives there are people we are always glad to see. They are a positive influence in our lives because we know they value us and have our best interests at heart. Whether they are family members, friends, or professional associates, they have a caring nature and genuine concern for us that enriches our lives.

What are the characteristics of these people?

First, they are positive, always looking for and expecting the best in others and in any situation. There is an unmistakable positive energy around them that is revealed in their demeanor and reflected in their words and actions.

Second, they are good listeners. They're more interested in us and what we have been doing (and are doing) than in their own lives. They are more likely to speak last than first. They always let you know that they value you and what you have to say.

Third, they are more apt to ask questions than give answers. They will be as enthusiastic for the ideas of others as for their own. In fact, they are more interested in finding the best solution to any issue than in having their own way.

Fourth, they take advantage of every opportunity to make even the smallest difference. They touch what needs to be loved, help heal whatever is broken, and make us more alive by being a part of our lives.

Fifth, they are always considerate and kind. Thoughtfulness and consideration for others are the bedrock of good manners.

PLAYBOOK EXERCISE

- Name three people who have good manners. How can you tell?
- Compare your life with the five characteristics listed at the end of this section. How do you stack up?

NEXT STEPS

- Pick one of the five characteristics and work on displaying it intentionally for a week.

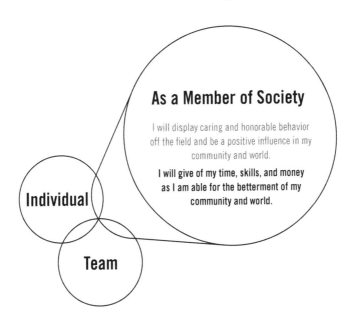

CHAPTER 9

Living The Code as a Member of Society

As a Member of Society

I will display caring and honorable behavior off the field and be a positive influence in my community and world.

I will give of my time, skills, and money as I am able for the betterment of my community and world.

Individual

Team

THE SECOND TENET

Everybody can be great because everybody can serve. You don't have to have a college degree to serve. You don't have to make your subject and your verb agree to serve. You don't have to know about

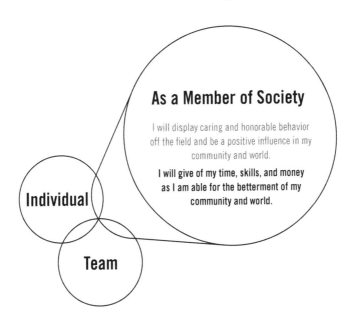

Plato and Aristotle to serve. You don't have to know Einstein's theory of relativity to serve. You don't have to know the second theory of thermodynamics in physics to serve. You only need a heart full of grace, a soul generated by love.

— Dr. Martin Luther King Jr.

By now it has become clear that the composing of our character has to include an awareness of and a participation in the community and world in which we live. Community service is not a value that everyone automatically assumes or shares. We will make no assumptions as we explore this tenet in the following way:

"I will give of my time, skills, and money as I am able for the betterment of my community and world."

9.1 From Passive Indifference to Active Participation
    To Become a Giver
    Members of the Human Family
    Finding Meaning
    The Meaning of Citizenship
    Our Religious Underpinnings
9.2 Discovering the Power of Giving
    Compassion Leads to Service
    Paying It Forward
    Giving "As I Am Able" Leads to Self-fulfillment

9.1 FROM PASSIVE INDIFFERENCE TO ACTIVE PARTICIPATION

TO BECOME A GIVER

NBA great Dikembe Mutombo came to the United States from the Congo to become a medical doctor. He was discovered by John Thompson on the Georgetown campus, and became one of the greatest players in NBA history. Mutombo, however, did not forget his calling to bring medicine to the Congo, and so with some of the wealth of his life and with tremendous work and energy, he has built a hospital in his native Kinshasa. It was the first new medical facility to be built in that part of Africa in over 40 years.

I asked Mutombo if it was difficult raising money for the hospital. I assumed the answer would be no because the NBA is filled with extremely wealthy individuals and because a person of Mutombo's stature would surely evoke an immediate positive response. He immediately said, "Yes, it was very difficult," and then told me a series of stories about players carrying over $100,000 on the airplane for gambling purposes but who would say no to his requests for his hospital. "Why was this?" I asked. His answer was simple: "Because they have no culture of giving."

His story reminded me of a time I was trying to raise money for a good cause. I went to a young man who was a member of a very wealthy family that owned one of the largest corporations in the country. When I asked for his support, his answer was startling: "Why should I give my money to someone else?" In other words, he was asking, "Why give anything to anyone?"

So, why should we give? How do we create a culture of giving?

PLAYBOOK EXERCISE

- How would you answer the "why give" question?
- Name three people you think are generous and three you think are not generous.
- Write down three reasons why you think people do not like to give.
- Write down three reasons why you think people like to give.

NEXT STEP

- Determine the percentage of your money that you give away. Could you increase it by 1%? By 2%? Determine what you would like to do now and in the future.

MEMBERS OF THE HUMAN FAMILY

When we are born we are completely dependent on others. We cannot feed ourselves or even roll over. Without the love and compassion of others we would never survive. We are not born alone or with wild animals, but with family. If we were born without the human environment—no language, no family, no nation, and none of the social progress or gains of history—could we really become a person? Or would we just remain an animal?

In fact, our lives are the accumulation of social relationships: our family, our relatives, our teammates, our coaches and teachers, our school friends, our neighborhood and our nation.

We are part of what is now called the global village. When we wake up we might wash with soap from Italy, shave with a razor from China, dry ourselves with a towel from England, put on clothes from France and shoes from South America, eat our breakfast cereal and bread from Kansas grain, drink Florida orange juice, and enjoy coffee from Colombia. As we become more aware, we realize that we are part of the whole human family, so in some sense all women are our sisters, and all men, our brothers.

One of the great challenges of growing up is in seeing the other person in this way. People of every nation and race and tribe begin by seeing themselves as somehow better than others. Provincialism is natural. Many people in Florida cannot imagine why anyone would live in North Dakota, and many in North Dakota cannot imagine why anyone would live in Florida.

This does not mean that we should not love our own people and our country best of all. We should love our own family heritage and our own country with a special feeling and devotion. Our family and our country are so much a part of us that they can give to us what no other relationship can give.

However, this love for our family and our country should open us up to the sacredness of all such relationships. We should be able to see that the love we share for our parents, brothers and sisters is the same as is shared by others everywhere, for their loved ones. We are poor citizens if we cannot see that others surely feel the same warmth and loyalty and pride and devotion to their native lands as we do to ours. Our love of our land should lead us to universal empathy for those in other countries. A good family and a good neighborhood and a good town all complement and fulfill each other. So, too, nationalism and internationalism should complement each other and lead to a better world for all.

FINDING MEANING

The Seattle SuperSonics professional basketball team was owned by the Ackerley family. When you walked into their corporate office there was a large wall on the right. This wall was completely empty except for one sentence painted in the middle: "You make a living by what you get. You make a life by what you give. —Winston Churchill."

The Ackerleys understood that meaningful life comes not from seeing how much you can get, but from living for a worthy purpose. We have within ourselves that greedy self that occupies the first room in the house that is our soul. But as we grow older, we add on more and more rooms so that our soul can expand and include those larger selves that seek not for themselves but for others. As we continue to grow, we move more and more from "I" to "we," and from "mine" to "our."

PLAYBOOK EXERCISE

- Do you agree with Winston Churchill?
- Do you think we have a moral responsibility to others? If so, where, if anywhere, would you draw the line: local, national, international?
- In what ways can that be shown in your life?

NEXT STEPS

- What is an interest of yours that you have been thinking of becoming more involved in but to which you have not yet responded?
- What would be the first step for you to take?

THE MEANING OF CITIZENSHIP

Most of the readers of this book are citizens of the United States. Citizenship means something; it means we have a civic duty to do more than live private lives. As we all know, the U.S. Constitution begins, "We the people of the United States, in order to form a more perfect union, ...to promote the general welfare..." It's not just about my welfare. The great weakness of many politicians is that they always seek to appeal to our self-interest, to my welfare, to "what's good for me," and not the *general* welfare, and they do this because they want us to like them and to support them. Just as there is no "I" in team, this nation's constitution literally begins with "We, the people."

During the First and Second World Wars, U.S. citizens were mobilized in ways that gave the country a sense of unity and purpose. Everyone made sacrifices and took on new responsibilities to aid the war effort. In the more modern era, President John F. Kennedy famously said in his inaugural address, "Ask not what your country can do for you; ask what you can do for your country." That is the spirit of service and working together for the common good. To demonstrate his commitment, President Kennedy began the Peace Corps as a vehicle for international volunteerism. This was (and is) an example of our nation seeking to live out its responsibilities to all peoples everywhere, of being a part of the family of nations.

OUR RELIGIOUS UNDERPINNINGS

This democracy that we cherish in the U. S.—like all Western culture and civilization—has as its underlying assumption a common ethic that we have inherited, whether we realize it or not. It's in our gene pool.

It doesn't matter if you go to a church, a synagogue, a mosque, or nowhere. The ethical assumption of our democracy has always been that we have a responsibility for one another, especially for those less fortunate. We are to clothe the naked, feed the hungry, take care of the sick, the aged, and the infirm because we're citizens, brothers and sisters, and we're in this together. It is important to remember that the moral and ethical duty for the common good was inherited from our various religious traditions and assumed by people of all faiths and of no faith, as the sub-soil of our democracy.

PLAYBOOK EXERCISE

- What do you think it means to be a citizen or resident of this country? What are your civic duties as a citizen?
- In what ways do you think the U. S. culture or that of your country reflects the various religious traditions?
- What are the sources of the values that are most important to you in your life?

NEXT STEPS

- Think about why the values you cherish are not being taught or passed on, as they were to you. Consider what you can do about that. Will you?

9.2 DISCOVERING THE POWER OF GIVING

COMPASSION LEADS TO SERVICE

We come together and work for the common good because we care. To work for the common good—to live out that civic responsibility we have as citizens—leads us to join together for countless activities and good works. We fight against cancer or other diseases; help out at an art museum, a symphony hall, or a sports stadium; build a home for a homeless person; respond to natural disaster cleanup or a neighbor's dying parent, all because we care.

We come together because we want to make things better. Margaret Mead said, "Never forget that a small group of dedicated people can change the world. It's all that ever has."

Ned Skinner, a well-known businessman in Seattle, was one of the great citizens of the city, always working for one cause or another. He once said something I love: "I never ask anyone for money when I don't think I'm doing them a favor because I'm giving them an opportunity to make their community better." Most people are hesitant to ask others for money, but not only did Skinner relish the opportunity, he did it with enthusiasm.

PAYING IT FORWARD

We join together because we know we can make a difference and because we know that others have come before us and made things possible for us. Althea Gibson said, "There's no champion who hasn't become a champion as a result of the efforts and support of someone else."

Echoing that thought, Maya Angelou carried it further when she said, "Our lives have already been paid for. I don't care who you are. Our lives have already been paid for. I don't care if your ancestors came here from Europe looking for religious freedom, or if they came from Ireland to dig the canals of the north, or if they came from the Caribbean to work in the industrial north, or if they came from Asia, to build the railroads of the west, or if they came in slave ships to work in the fields of the south. Our lives have already been paid for. When you realize that, when you internalize that just one little bit, you stand up straighter, and you prepare to pay for one yet to come."

And so, we must look inside ourselves. We must determine that our life will make a difference. We cannot look for a life of ease and isolation as if the only reason we are here is to see how much we can get! We must let our hearts be open to the difficulties, the struggles, the pain of others, so that the empathy we feel may shape us, move us, and lead us to greater caring. We must be willing to walk with others and share their burdens so that we may lighten their load and give hope to their despair.

Our common creed must be, "He ain't heavy; he's my brother. She ain't heavy; she's my sister." In our daily lives we must do more than random acts of kindness. We must let the fabric of our lives reflect and radiate a desire to make this a better world. In other words, we must live fully and completely. If we live life, love life, and give life, we will be alive as never before. Most importantly, we'll all have a better community and a better world.

PLAYBOOK EXERCISE

- Who has "paid for you" and helped you become the person you are today?
- What problems in your community or in the world have you responded to? What is it that blocks you from responding more often?

NEXT STEPS

- Write out three community-based goals for yourself for the coming year. They should be three goals that will help you make a difference in the lives of those nearby or far away.

GIVING "AS I AM ABLE" LEADS TO SELF-FULFILLMENT

In Israel, the Jordan River flows into the Sea of Galilee and continues down to the Dead Sea. The Dead Sea is so named because there is no life in it. Nothing flows out of the Dead Sea; it only receives. It is a parable of life: Life comes by giving, not by taking.

"As I am able" is something that each person must define for himself or herself. It may mean giving up one Saturday morning—or many. It may mean giving up one dollar—or many dollars. The life that flows into us in innumerable ways must also flow out of us. The important thing is that we have a common understanding: We all have a responsibility for the betterment of our world, and that responsibility begins with small steps and small actions.

Some people are not used to giving money away. But two things are true: Giving helps the giver, and giving helps the receiver. Whenever we give a gift, we feel better than before. Whenever we respond to a need, we feel better. Why? Because we become more of a person, and our sense of self, of who we are, is developed. In other words, rather than just trying to live alone and selfishly get all we can for ourselves, when we reach out and respond to our neighbors in need, we find our own lives enriched.

When we respond and reach out, we grow and become more than we were before. We also have a sense of accomplishment, which will lead us to do additional things in the future.

The goal we are always working toward is that of developing a generous heart and a generous spirit, which will result in asking ourselves if we are doing all we can and what the next step is.

Have you thought about the skills you have that would benefit others? We often think of "skills" as those superior abilities that only some have. In fact, we all have many skills: the skill of being a friend, of listening to another, of helping out by participating in a program or project, or of helping a younger person with a subject or sport. We all have many more skills to offer to others than we first recognize.

PLAYBOOK EXERCISE

- When have you felt the best as the result of serving others?
- What skills do you have? What would others say?
- How can you help others have a sense of responsibility for others?

NEXT STEPS

- What is the one thing you care most about in the world? What is the next step you can take to work on that issue?
- What other individuals or groups can you invite to join with you?

FINAL THOUGHTS

We began this book by recalling Montaigne's words, "Our duty is not to compose books but our character, and to win peace, not in war, but in our lives. Our great and glorious accomplishment is to live the right way." As we come to the end, we want to take a moment to sum up all that we have tried to say along the way.

We can ask the question, "What is good character?"

Character is the result of all the choices we make, whether for good or ill, throughout our lives. Our character is never finally completed; it is made and remade by all the choices we face every day of our lives. There is nothing theoretical about our character. It is not some ideal to which we aspire; it is the concrete result of the choices we make, the habits we practice, the words we speak, and the actions we demonstrate for others to see.

Theologian Harry Emerson Fosdick, contemplating the ways in which people he admired responded to the challenges of life, wrote: "They act as though character, not happiness, were the end of life ... as though moral quality were the purpose of creation."

Character is that holy of holies within each person. It is who you are. It is not just reputation because that can be wrong. It is who you really are. We know great character when we see it and when it is lived. It is shown in people who have noble traits that have been developed through time, tested and refined. It is shown in people whose word is their bond and whose handshake is worth more than any legal document. It is shown in people who have the courage to speak the truth as they know it in any circumstance, and who will listen to others with respect and an open mind. It is shown in people whose hearts cherish family, friends, home, and places of meaning. It shines through the soul that holds onto these elements of character and nurtures them. Our character is the assimilation of all those big words: honor, truth, duty, kindness, discipline, courage, fortitude, sacrifice, and love.

When we do not have the necessary inner strength of character, these virtues will dry up and disappear. Those who are weak will not be able to maintain them. Character is like any garden: if it is not tended and nurtured, it will soon be overrun with weeds and all sorts of undesirable growth. It is never finished; with each new day there is always work to be done.

Life is a mystery beyond our understanding. We all have to make choices every day, and those choices are the playing field for determining what kind of person we'll become. There is no guaranteed result for the choices we make. At the end of the day we're not automatically punished or rewarded for what we've done. In fact, some sort of temporary happiness is usually guaranteed for making the less noble or the wrong choice. Virtue, goodness, and love are their own rewards, and in pursuing them, we develop the best within us.

It's also true that we so often see the meaning of things in their opposites. You see the meaning of a brave person in the action of a coward; you see the meaning of a good person in the action of a bad one; you see honor when dishonor is shown, or kindness when meanness is evident. It is in times of trial that character is often best revealed and strengthened, for it is how we treat both triumph and disaster that reveals who we are and who we are becoming.

Character, then, is not something that comes automatically, or without thinking, or without effort. One of the moral laws of the universe that binds life together is that nothing worthwhile is achieved or maintained except at a price. Building a relationship, a business, or even a nation requires never-ending effort, sacrifice, and patience. Love is never free. It has many demands: kindness, compassion, and forgiveness. Along with its joys and profound pleasures, it always brings heartbreak and grief, if only at the end. Life is not about winning the lottery; it is about opportunity and challenge day in and day out, about struggle and difficulty, about victories and defeats, about the will to persevere, as

Kipling says, when there is nothing in you that says to continue except the will that says to hold on! Nothing that is worthwhile is ever cheap. It is character that recognizes the nature of life; it embraces it and joins in, knowing the inevitable defeats and heartbreaks that will come, but still willing to participate and to suffer for the joys and pleasures that it brings as well.

Our lives and our choices are the framework on which we build our character. Duty is one of those great words of character. But duty is only a word until someone performs it. How we bear all of life's difficulties is a measure of our sense of duty. Do we curse the darkness, or do we get up, go find a candle, and light it? Our duty is to live fully and completely to the best of our abilities, without sadness and defeat and without surrender. Our duty is not to be happy (as Fosdick said) but to live fearlessly and courageously in the face of whatever comes our way.

There was a man who did not go to a family wedding for what he thought was a very good reason: It was the opening day of duck season. The fact that he had shot thousands of ducks in the past and would shoot thousands more did not matter. He wouldn't skip duck hunting. It was a selfish act consistent with who he was; he had a serious character deficiency. However, over the years, he grew, and to the surprise and amazement of many, that selfishness that had dominated his younger and middle years was overtaken by a love for his family and the shifting of his perspectives and priorities. When he died in his 90s he was not the person who had gone duck hunting 45 years earlier. Like him, we all have areas to work on, ways to learn to love more, forgive more, to cherish more.

I remember two stories Mr. Ashburn related on more than one occasion. The first is about Captain Robert Scott who led two unsuccessful attempts to be the first person to get to the South Pole. During the second try, as the group got within 800 miles or so, Captain Scott selected a few people to go with him on the final push. They got there, discovered another group had beaten them, and headed back.

A terrible blizzard that lasted a long time interrupted their return and they hunkered down in a tent. At one point, a man named Oates realized that they were going to run out of food. He thought the others had a better chance of survival without him. He announced that "I am just going outside and may be some time," and he walked off into the storm and to his death. What could possibly represent greater character or greater desire to help the team?

When food ran out, and it was apparent the end was only days away, Captain Scott, knowing they would eventually be found, wrote some final words:

We took risks, we knew we took them; things have come out against us, and therefore we have no cause for complaint but bow to the will of Providence, determined still to do our best to the last ...

He also wrote letters to his mother, wife, and to the families of his companions. To the mother of one he wrote:

My dear Mrs. Bowers,

I am afraid this will reach you after one of the heaviest blows of your life. I write when we are very near the end of our journey, and I am finishing it in the company of two noble gallant gentlemen. One of these is your son. He had come to be one of my closest and soundest friends, and I appreciate his wonderful upright nature, his ability and energy. As the troubles have thickened, his dauntless spirit ever shone brighter, and he has remained cheerful, hopeful, and indomitable to the end.

My whole heart goes out in pity to you.

Within a few days later they had all died. Scott's words, however, waited to be discovered, "...he has remained cheerful, hopeful, and indomitable to the end."

Our character reflects how we live, what we live for, and how we die. Mr. Ashburn often referred to Edmond Rostand's play *Cyrano de Bergerac*. De Bergerac was a proud but tragic figure. The symbol of his personal honor and integrity, of who he was, was a white plume that he wore in his hat. In one of the final scenes, de Bergerac is dying and hallucinating. He sees death coming, and he says:

"Let him come. He'll find me on my feet, sword in hand...What's that you say? Hopeless. Ha, very well. A man doesn't fight merely to win, no, no, better to know one fights in vain...

I recognize you—all my old enemies. Lying. Compromise. Prejudice. Cowardice. Silliness ... Vanity. (*He flails his sword wildly in the air.*)... Never mind—I'll fight on.... You would try to take everything from me, all my glory,... but when I enter heaven... I'll take one thing with me, without a wrinkle or a spot—and that is my white plume."

Our character is our sacred white plume. We compose it every day of our lives, we defend it with all our energy and effort, and we carry it to our death.

Appendix  **A**

About the Author

Author Frederick B. Northup was graduated from Sewanee: The University of the South and began his professional career as a high school French teacher and coach at the McCallie School in Chattanooga, Tennessee, was a tennis pro at the Midtown Tennis Club in New York while attending the General Theological Seminary, then served the Episcopal church as a priest for 25 years, from Memphis to Paris to New York to Louisiana to Seattle, where he was dean of St. Mark's Cathedral, the largest Episcopal congregation in the Northwest. He has coached a number of teams at different levels in several sports and served in leadership positions on a variety of nonprofit boards. In 1998, Fred took early retirement and founded Athletes for a Better World, an international nonprofit organization with a mission to develop character, teamwork, and citizenship in athletes. He has received the endorsement of numerous national figures in sports including the legendary John Wooden, in whose name an annual award is given to one professional and one collegiate athlete.

Appendix B

The ABW Team

BRAD CATHERMAN, EXECUTIVE DIRECTOR

Collaborator Brad Catherman's corporate marketing and sales management career included work for Turner Broadcasting Sports Promotions and other blue chip brands. Prior to the 1996 Olympic Games held in Atlanta, he was a part of the media relations group during the international bid process. Brad has also been associated with nonprofit companies and organizations such as Special Olympics as a development executive, board member and volunteer. His athletic career included a (very) brief free agency with the Dallas Cowboys as a wide receiver, as a sprinter in the National Bicycling Championships kilometer time trial, and as a multi-time winner of the coveted Presidential Physical Fitness Award. Brad's humorous and inspirational Hollywood memoir entitled *Open-field Running: The Adventure of Selling a Screenplay* details winning awards in six screenwriting contests on his way to his first film production deal. He was a multi-sport athlete at Marist School prep in Atlanta where he achieved the rank of Cadet Major in the Air Force JROTC program, and he later co-founded the Blue & Gold Athletics Circle Hall of Fame. Brad received a Bachelor of Science in psychology from Emory University where he was later invited to throw out the first pitch during dedication ceremonies of the baseball field to honor NCAA visionary athletic director and mentor "Doc" Partin. He received a Master of

Science in Sports Administration of the Business School of St. Thomas University/Miami where he was a graduate assistant in the university marketing department. Brad spent many years as a youth coach to his son, Andy, who excelled in football, baseball, basketball, track, soccer, golf, and wrestling.

Brad's wife Julie remains his lighthouse in a sea of changing times, helping to point the way in life through her unconditional love. He is the richer for her inner character that she demonstrates daily.

ATHLETES FOR A BETTER WORLD BOARD OF DIRECTORS

RYAN ADLER, Director, Stamford, CT
Finance, Royal Bank of Scotland

TAZ ANDERSON, Director, Atlanta, GA
Taz L. Anderson Realty Company

HENRY BAUER, Director, Atlanta, GA
Attorney

LEE BIRDSONG, Board Vice Chair, Atlanta, GA
Communicator, Southern Company

FLO BRYAN, Director, Atlanta, GA
Senior Vice President, Cause and Diversity Marketing, CSE

JAY DAVIS, Director, Atlanta, GA
Chairman/CEO, National Distributing Company

DANIELLE DONEHEW, Director, Atlanta, GA
Executive Director, Women's Basketball Coaches Association

VINCENT J. DOOLEY, Honorary Lifetime Member, Athens, GA
Member, College Football Hall of Fame

DAVID EARLE, Director, Rowayton, CT
Managing Partner, Edvise Partners

DICK ENERSEN, Chair Emeritus, Sausalito, CA
Philanthropist, The Enersen Foundation

BILLY ESPY, Board Chair, Atlanta, GA
Real Estate Developer, The Espy Company

JOHN HOERSTER, Chair Emeritus, Seattle, WA
Attorney, Saltchuk Resources

HEATHER KARVIS, Director, Atlanta, GA
Dean, Teacher and Coach, The Westminster Schools

SALLY LEYMAN, Board Secretary, Cincinnati, OH
Middle School Coach, Seven Hills School

MONISHA LONGACRE, Director, Atlanta, GA
Chief Product Officer, PlayOn! Sports / NFHS Network

FRED NORTHUP, Board President, Asheville, NC
Founder of ABW

EARL RAHN, Director, Tampa, FL
Owner, NewSouth Windows & Doors

JIM SHELTON, Director, Atlanta, GA
Real Estate Investor, Carter & Assoc.

CHRIS TIDWELL, Director, Atlanta, GA
Principal/Architect, HDR, Inc.

P J WADE, Board Treasurer, Atlanta, GA
Financial Operations Manager, Children's Healthcare of Atlanta

JOE WALTON, Director, Atlanta, GA
Senior Director of Sales, Comcast Business

APPENDIX C

The Coach Wooden Citizenship Cup

The Coach Wooden Citizenship Cup is named in honor of John Wooden, a man who embodied the characteristics of an athlete of excellence. The Wooden Cup is presented to two distinguished athletes, one professional and one collegiate, for their character and leadership both on and off the field and for their contributions to sport and to society.

To be nominated for The Wooden Cup, an athlete must:

- Train with a disciplined, consistent work ethic
- Demonstrate fair play and superior sportsmanship
- Develop positive, supportive relationships with teammates and coaches
- Win or lose with grace and dignity
- Make a significant difference in the community and world

Nominations for the cup are solicited from more than 2,000 colleges and universities, and professional athletes are considered from every sport. The college nominations are screened by three different committees: the initial screening committee, which narrows the large number of nominations; the National Electors, a geographically balanced group of approximately 100 voters from throughout the United States who vote from the screened list of candidates; and College Football Hall of Fame Coach and former University of Georgia Athletics Director Vince Dooley chairs the committee that makes the final decision.

THE RECIPIENTS OF THE COACH WOODEN CITIZENSHIP CUP HAVE BEEN:

2015	Professional Level	Shannon Miller, gymnastics
	College Level	Madeline Buckley, William Smith College

2014	Professional Level	Drew Brees, football
	College Level	Dau Jok, University of Pennsylvania

2013	Professional Level	Jack Nicklaus, golf
	College Level	**Nathanael Franks, University of Arkansas**

2012	Professional Level	Pat Summitt, women's basketball coach
	College Level	Aleca Hughes, Yale University

2011	Professional Level	Dikembe Mutombo, basketball
	College Level	Quinton Carter, University of Oklahoma

2010	Professional Level	Mia Hamm, soccer
	College Level	Zak Boggs, University of South Florida

2009	Professional Level	Cal Ripken Jr., baseball
	College Level	Tim Tebow, University of Florida

2008	Professional Level	Andrea Yaeger, tennis
	College Level	Will Bruce, Williams College

2007	Professional Level	John Lynch, football
	College Level	Anna Key, University of California

2006	Professional Level	John Smoltz, baseball
	College Level	Jacqueline DuBois, University of Oklahoma

2005	Professional Level	Peyton Manning, football
	College Level	William Betz, Brigham Young University

COACH WOODEN CITIZENSHIP CUP ADVISORY COMMITTEE

VINCENT J. DOOLEY, Chair
College Football Hall of Fame

GINGER ACKERLEY
Former owner, Seattle SuperSonics

CHUCK ARMSTRONG
President, Seattle Mariners

CHARLES BATTLE
Olympic Consultant

KATHY JOHNSON CLARKE
Olympic Gold Medalist

DONNA DE VARONA
Olympic Gold Medalist

MIKE FLOOD
Community Relations, Seattle Seahawks

KENDRA JONES
The Gates Foundation

ARCHIE MANNING
Hall of Fame quarterback

NATE McMILLAN
Former NBA great and coach

BILLY PAYNE
Chairman, Augusta National

CAL RIPKEN, JR.
  Hall of Fame, baseball

JOHN SMOLTZ
  Hall of Fame, baseball

GENE STALLINGS
  Former Head Football Coach, University of Alabama

ROBERT TRUMP
  Commercial Real Estate

JAMAAL WILKES
  NBA Hall of Fame

Made in the USA
Charleston, SC
13 October 2016